MACARTHUR BIBLE STUDIES

RUTH & ESTHER

Women of Faith, Bravery and Hope

JOHN
MACARTHUR

Ruth and Esther
MacArthur Bible Studies

John MacArthur
"Unleashing God's Truth, One Verse at a Time®"
"Unleashing God's Truth, One Verse at a Time" is a trademark of Grace to You. All rights reserved.

Scripture passages taken from:
The Holy Bible, *New King James Version*
© 1979, 1980, 1982 by Thomas Nelson. All rights reserved.

Cover Art by The Puckett Group.
Interior design and composition by Design Corps, Batavia, IL.

Produced with the assistance of the Livingstone Corporation. Project staff include Dave Veerman, Christopher D. Hudson, and Amber Rae.

Project editor: Len Woods

ISBN-13: 978-0-8499-5546-4
All rights reserved. *Printed in the United States of America.*

13 14 15   QG   30 29 28

Ruth and Esther
Table of Contents

THE BOOK OF RUTH

Introduction

Ancient versions and modern translations consistently entitle this book after Ruth the Moabitess the heroine, who is mentioned by name twelve times (1:4—4:13). Only two Old Testament books receive their names from women—Ruth and Esther. The Old Testament does not again refer to Ruth, while the New Testament mentions her just once—in the context of Christ's genealogy (Matthew 1:5; see Ruth 4:18–22). The name "Ruth" most likely comes from a Moabite or Hebrew word meaning "friendship." Ruth arrived in Bethlehem as a foreigner (2:10), became a maidservant (2:13), married wealthy Boaz (4:13), and is listed in the physical lineage of Christ (Matthew 1:5).

Author and Date

Jewish tradition credits Samuel as the author of this book, which is plausible since he did not die until after he had anointed David as God's chosen king (1 Samuel 16:6–13; 25:1). Neither the internal features nor external testimony, however, conclusively identifies the writer. This exquisite story most likely appeared shortly before or during David's reign of Israel (1011–971 B.C.), since David is mentioned (4:17, 22) but not Solomon. The German author, Goethe reportedly labeled this piece of anonymous but unexcelled literature as "the loveliest, complete work on a small scale." What Venus is to statuary and the Mona Lisa is to paintings, Ruth is to literature.

Background and Setting

Aside from Bethlehem (1:1), Moab (the perennial enemy of Israel, situated east of the Dead Sea) stands as the only other mentioned geographic/national entity (1:1–2). This country originated when Lot fathered Moab by an incestuous union with his oldest daughter (Genesis 19:37). Centuries later the Jews encountered opposition from Balak, king of Moab, through the prophet Balaam (Numbers 22–25). For eighteen years Moab oppressed Israel during the period of the judges (Judges 3:12–30). Saul defeated the Moabites (1 Samuel 14:47), while David seemed to enjoy a peaceful relationship with them (1 Samuel 22:3, 4). Later, Moab again troubled Israel (2 Kings 3:5–27; Ezra 9:1). Because of Moab's idolatrous worship of Chemosh (1 Kings 11:7, 33; 2 Kings 23:13) and its opposition to Israel, God cursed Moab (Isaiah 15–16; Jeremiah 48; Ezekiel 25:8–11; Amos 2:1–3).

The story of Ruth occurred in the days "when the judges ruled" Israel (Ruth 1:1)—1370 to 1041 B.C. (Judges 2:16–19)—and thus bridges the time from the judges to Israel's monarchy. God used a famine in the land of Judah (Ruth 1:1) to set in motion this beautiful drama, although the famine does not receive mention in Judges, which causes difficulty in dating the events of Ruth. By working backward in time from the well-known dates of David's reign (1011–971 B.C.), however, the time period of Ruth would most likely be during the judgeship of Jair, 1126–1105 B.C. (Judges 10:3–5).

Ruth covers about eleven or twelve years according to the following outline: (1) 1:1–18, ten years in Moab (1:4); (2) 1:19—2:23, two months (mid-April to mid-June) in Boaz's field (1:22; 2:23); (3) 3:1–18, one day in Bethlehem and one night at the threshing floor; (4) 4:1–22, about one year in Bethlehem.

Historical and Theological Themes

All eighty-five verses of Ruth have been accepted as canonical by the Jews. Along with Song of Solomon, Esther, Ecclesiastes, and Lamentations, Ruth stands with the Old Testament books of the Megilloth or "five scrolls." Rabbis read these books in the synagogue on five special occasions during the year— Ruth being read at Pentecost due to the harvest scenes of Ruth 2–3.

Genealogically, Ruth looks back almost nine hundred years to events in the time of Jacob (4:11) and forward about one hundred years to the coming reign of David (4:17, 22). While Joshua and Judges emphasize the legacy of the nation and their land of promise, Ruth focuses on the lineage of David back to the Patriarchal era.

At least seven major theological themes emerge in Ruth. First, Ruth the Moabitess illustrates that God's redemptive plan extended beyond the Jews to Gentiles (2:12). Second, Ruth demonstrates that women are coheirs with men of God's salvation grace (see 1 Peter 3:7). Third, Ruth portrays the virtuous woman of Proverbs 31:10 (see 3:11). Fourth, Ruth describes God's sovereign (1:6; 4:13) and providential care (2:3) of seemingly unimportant people at apparently insignificant times which later prove to be monumentally crucial to accomplishing God's will. Fifth, Ruth along with Tamar (Genesis 38), Rahab (Joshua 2), and Bathsheba (2 Samuel 11–12) stand in the genealogy of the Messianic line (4:17, 22; see Matthew 1:5). Sixth, Boaz, as a type of Christ, becomes Ruth's kinsman-redeemer (4:1–12). Finally, David's right (and thus Christ's right) to the throne of Israel is traced back to Judah (4:18–22; see Genesis 49:8–12).

Interpretive Challenges

Ruth should be understood as a true historical account. The reliable facts surrounding Ruth, in addition to its complete compatibility with Judges plus 1 and 2 Samuel, confirm the book's authenticity. Some individual difficulties require careful attention, however.

First, how could Ruth worship at the tabernacle then in Shiloh (1 Samuel 4:4), since Deuteronomy 23:3 expressly forbids Moabites from entering the assembly for ten generations? The Jews entered the land in about 1405 B.C., and Ruth was not born until approximately 1150 B.C.; thus, she represented at least the eleventh generation (probably later) if the time limitation ended at ten generations. If "ten generations" was an idiom meaning "forever" as Nehemiah 13:1 implies, then Ruth would be like the foreigner of Isaiah 56:1–8 who joined himself to the Lord (Ruth 1:16), thus gaining entrance to the assembly.

Second, are there not immoral overtones to Boaz and Ruth spending the night together before marriage (3:3–18)? Ruth engaged in a common ancient Near Eastern custom by asking Boaz to take her for his wife as symbolically pictured by throwing a garment over the intended woman (3:9), just as Yahweh spread His garment over Israel (Ezekiel 16:8). The text does not even hint at the slightest moral impropriety, noting that Ruth slept at Boaz's feet (Ruth 3:14). Thus, Boaz became God's answer to his own earlier prayer for Ruth (2:12).

Third, would not the levirate principle of Deuteronomy 25:5–6 lead to incest or polygamy if the nearest relative were already married? God would not design a good plan to involve the grossest of immoralities punishable by death. It is to be assumed that the implementation of Deuteronomy 25:5–6 could involve only the nearest relative who was eligible for marriage as qualified by other stipulations of the law.

Fourth, was not marriage to a Moabitess strictly forbidden by the law? The nations or people to whom marriage was prohibited were those possessing the land that Israel would enter (Exodus 34:16; Deuteronomy 7:1–3; Joshua 23:12), and that group did not include Moab (see Deuteronomy 7:1). Further, Ruth, a devout proselyte to Yahweh (Ruth 1:16–17), was not a pagan worshiper of Chemosh—Moab's chief deity (see later problems in Ezra 9:1–2 and Nehemiah 13:23–25).

Ruth's Decision

Opening Thought

1) Think back over your life and list two or three of the most memorable examples of loyalty or commitment you've ever seen.

_____

_____

_____

2) What made these events so remarkable?

_____

_____

_____

3) What is the secret (if there is one) to unswerving devotion?

_____

_____

_____

4) Why are in-law relationships commonly the brunt of harsh joking and the source of so much tension?

_____

_____

_____

_____

Background of the Passage

Like a sparkling diamond set against a black velvet background, Ruth's life and story stand in sharp contrast to one of Israel's darkest times. Ruth lived during the period of the judges (1400–1050 B.C.), a time characterized by faithlessness and lawlessness. Judges 21:25 sums up the era well: "In those days there was no king in Israel; everyone did what was right in his own eyes."

Ruth was a rare exception. A Moabite by birth, she married an Israelite man who had come with his entire family to her country because of a severe famine in Israel. It is likely that Ruth came to faith in Yahweh because of the influence of her Jewish husband and in-laws. When her husband and father-in-law both died, Ruth faced a tough decision: remain in her homeland or return to Israel with her mother-in-law.

Defying her times, Ruth chose to stick by the side of her mother-in-law, Naomi. The result is a fascinating story of love, commitment, and redemption. The Old Testament Book of Ruth not only gives us insights into ancient Israelite customs, it also is strongly permeated by the sovereignty of God on behalf of Israel: (1) actually for good (2:12; 4:12–14); (2) perceived by Naomi for bad (1:13, 21); (3) in the context of prayer/blessing (1:8–9, 17; 2:4, 12, 20; 3:10, 13; 4:11). It furthermore demonstrates the truth of 2 Chronicles 16:9: "For the eyes of the LORD run to and fro throughout the whole earth, to show Himself strong on behalf of those whose heart is loyal to Him." Because of her selflessness, Ruth became the wife of Boaz and the great-grandmother of King David. Because of her faithfulness, Ruth gained a privileged position in the lineage of Christ!

Bible Passage

Read 1:1–22, noting the key words and definitions to the right of the passage.

Ruth 1:1–22

¹ *Now it came to pass, in the days when the judges ruled, that there was a famine in the land. And a certain man of Bethlehem, Judah, went to dwell in the country of Moab, he and his wife and his two sons.*

² *The name of the man was Elimelech, the name*

famine (v. 1)—similar to the days of Abraham (Genesis 12), Isaac (Genesis 26), and Jacob (Genesis 46); it is unclear whether or not this famine was God's judgment (see 1 Kings 17–18, esp. 18:2)

Bethlehem, Judah (v. 1)— Bethlehem ("house of bread") lies

of his wife was Naomi, and the names of his two sons were Mahlon and Chilion—Ephrathites of Bethlehem, Judah. And they went to the country of Moab and remained there.

3 Then Elimelech, Naomi's husband, died; and she was left, and her two sons.

4 Now they took wives of the women of Moab: the name of the one was Orpah, and the name of the other Ruth. And they dwelt there about ten years.

5 Then both Mahlon and Chilion also died; so the woman survived her two sons and her husband.

6 Then she arose with her daughters-in-law that she might return from the country of Moab, for she had heard in the country of Moab that the LORD had visited His people by giving them bread.

7 Therefore she went out from the place where she was, and her two daughters-in-law with her; and they went on the way to return to the land of Judah.

8 And Naomi said to her two daughters-in-law, "Go, return each to her mother's house. The Lord deal kindly with you, as you have dealt with the dead and with me.

9 The LORD grant that you may find rest, each in the house of her husband." Then she kissed them, and they lifted up their voices and wept.

10 And they said to her, "Surely we will return with you to your people."

11 But Naomi said, "Turn back, my daughters; why will you go with me? Are there still sons in my womb, that they may be your husbands?

12 Turn back, my daughters, go—for I am too old to have a husband. If I should say I have hope, if I should have a husband tonight and should also bear sons,

13 would you wait for them till they were grown? Would you restrain yourselves from having husbands? No, my daughters; for it grieves me very much for your sakes that the hand of the LORD has gone out against me!"

in the territory given to the tribe of Judah (Joshua 15) about six miles south of Jerusalem.

dwell (v. 1)—Elimelech intended to live temporarily in Moab as a resident alien until the famine passed.

Elimelech (v. 2)—His name means "my God is king," signifying a devout commitment to the God of Israel. Most likely, he was a prominent man in the community whose brothers might have included the unnamed close relative and Boaz (see 4:3).

Naomi (v. 2)—Her name means "pleasant."

Mahlon and Chilion (v. 2)—Their names mean "sick" and "pining," respectively.

Ephrathites (v. 2)—a title used of people who lived in the area more anciently known as Ephrath (Genesis 35:16, 19; 48:7) or Ephrathah (Ruth 4:11; Micah 5:2) but later more prominently called Bethlehem (Ruth 1:1)

Orpah (v. 4)—Her name means "stubborn."

Ruth (v. 4)—Her name means "friendship."

about ten years (v. 4)—This period would seem to include the entire time of Naomi's residency in Moab.

the woman survived (v. 5)—Naomi, a widow in Moab whose two sons had also died, believed that the Lord had afflicted her with bitter days until she would die (1:13, 20–21). No reason for the death of these three men in her life is given.

the LORD had visited His people (v. 6)—The Lord had sent rain to break the famine.

14 Then they lifted up their voices and wept again; and Orpah kissed her mother-in-law, but Ruth clung to her.

15 And she said, "Look, your sister-in-law has gone back to her people and to her gods; return after your sister-in-law."

16 But Ruth said:

"Entreat me not to leave you,
Or to turn back from following after you;
For wherever you go, I will go;
And wherever you lodge, I will lodge;
Your people shall be my people,
And your God, my God.

17 Where you die, I will die,
And there will I be buried.
The LORD do so to me, and more also,
If anything but death parts you and me."

18 When she saw that she was determined to go with her, she stopped speaking to her.

19 Now the two of them went until they came to Bethlehem. And it happened, when they had come to Bethlehem, that all the city was excited because of them; and the women said, "Is this Naomi?"

20 But she said to them, "Do not call me Naomi; call me Mara, for the Almighty has dealt very bitterly with me.

21 I went out full, and the LORD has brought me home again empty. Why do you call me Naomi, since the LORD has testified against me, and the Almighty has afflicted me?"

22 So Naomi returned, and Ruth the Moabitess her daughter-in-law with her, who returned from the country of Moab. Now they came to Bethlehem at the beginning of barley harvest.

Go, return (v. 8)—Naomi graciously encouraged her two daughters-in-law to return to their homes (1:8) and to remarry (1:9), but they emotionally insisted on going to Jerusalem with her (1:10).

Are there still sons in my womb (v. 11)—Naomi selflessly reasoned a second time for their return because she would be unable to provide them with new husbands. If Orpah and Ruth waited, they would most likely have become as old as Naomi was then before they could remarry.

I am too old (v. 12)—Naomi was probably over fifty.

the hand of the Lord (v. 13)—a figure of speech that describes the Lord's work; God is spirit and therefore does not have a literal hand

her gods (v. 15)—refers to Chemosh, the chief Moabite deity, who required child sacrifice

And your God, my God (v. 16)—This testimony evidenced Ruth's conversion from worshiping Chemosh to Yahweh of Israel.

they came to Bethlehem (v. 19)—A trip from Moab (at least 60–75 miles) would have taken about 7–10 days. Having descended about 4,500 feet from Moab into the Jordan Valley, they then ascended 3,750 feet through the hills of Judea.

all the city (v. 19)—Naomi had been well known in her prior residency (see Ephrathites of Bethlehem, Ruth 1:2). The question, "Is this Naomi?" most likely reflected the hard life of the last decade and the toll that it took on her appearance.

Naomi . . . Mara; full . . . empty (vv. 20–21)—Naomi's outlook on life, although grounded in God's sovereignty, was not hopeful; thus she asked to be renamed Mara, which means "bitter." Her experiences were similar to Job's (Job 1–2), but her perspective resembled that of Job's wife (Job 2:9–10). In reality, Naomi had a full harvest prospect, Ruth plus Boaz, and the hope of God's future blessing.

Ruth, the Moabitess (v. 22) —This title also appears at 2:2, 21; 4:5, 10. Ruth stands out as a foretaste of future Gentile conversions (see Romans 11).

at the beginning of barley harvest (v. 22)—normally the middle to the end of April

Understanding the Text

5) Why did Elimelech take his family to Moab? Was this an act of wisdom and obedience or a demonstration of a weak faith? Why?

_____

_____

_____

_____

(verses to consider: Genesis 12, 26, 46)

6) Why is it significant that the sons of Elimelech married Moabite women?

_____

_____

_____

_____

7) Why did Naomi discourage Ruth and Orpah from accompanying her to Judah?

_____

_____

_____

_____

8) Ruth's expression of allegiance is legendary (and often recited in marriage ceremonies). What specific promises did she make?

_____

_____

_____

_____

9) What evidence is there that Ruth had become a believer in the one true God?

_____

_____

_____

_____

10) How would you describe Naomi's mood upon her return to Bethlehem? Were her complaints legitimate?

_____

_____

_____

_____

Cross-Reference

Read Judges 2:6–23 to get a feel for the times in which Ruth and Naomi lived.

⁶ *And when Joshua had dismissed the people, the children of Israel went each to his own inheritance to possess the land.*

⁷ *So the people served the LORD all the days of Joshua, and all the days of the elders who outlived Joshua, who had seen all the great works of the LORD which He had done for Israel.*

⁸ *Now Joshua the son of Nun, the servant of the LORD, died when he was one hundred and ten years old.*

⁹ And they buried him within the border of his inheritance at Timnath Heres, in the mountains of Ephraim, on the north side of Mount Gaash.

¹⁰ When all that generation had been gathered to their fathers, another generation arose after them who did not know the LORD nor the work which He had done for Israel.

¹¹ Then the children of Israel did evil in the sight of the LORD, and served the Baals;

¹² and they forsook the LORD God of their fathers, who had brought them out of the land of Egypt; and they followed other gods from among the gods of the people who were all around them, and they bowed down to them; and they provoked the LORD to anger.

¹³ They forsook the LORD and served Baal and the Ashtoreths.

¹⁴ And the anger of the LORD was hot against Israel. So He delivered them into the hands of plunderers who despoiled them; and He sold them into the hands of their enemies all around, so that they could no longer stand before their enemies.

¹⁵ Wherever they went out, the hand of the LORD was against them for calamity, as the LORD had said, and as the LORD had sworn to them. And they were greatly distressed.

¹⁶ Nevertheless, the LORD raised up judges who delivered them out of the hand of those who plundered them.

¹⁷ Yet they would not listen to their judges, but they played the harlot with other gods, and bowed down to them. They turned quickly from the way in which their fathers walked, in obeying the commandments of the LORD; they did not do so.

¹⁸ And when the LORD raised up judges for them, the LORD was with the judge and delivered them out of the hand of their enemies all the days of the judge; for the LORD was moved to pity by their groaning because of those who oppressed them and harassed them.

¹⁹ And it came to pass, when the judge was dead, that they reverted and behaved more corruptly than their fathers, by following other gods, to serve them and bow down to them. They did not cease from their own doings nor from their stubborn way.

²⁰ Then the anger of the LORD was hot against Israel; and He said, "Because this nation has transgressed My covenant which I commanded their fathers, and has not heeded My voice,

²¹ I also will no longer drive out before them any of the nations which Joshua left when he died,

²² so that through them I may test Israel, whether they will keep the ways of the LORD, to walk in them as their fathers kept them, or not."

²³ Therefore the LORD left those nations, without driving them out immediately; nor did He deliver them into the hand of Joshua.

Exploring the Meaning

11) How does Ruth's commitment to Naomi stand in contrast to the spirit of the times? How is Ruth's personal spiritual journey different than the religious trajectory of the nation of Israel?

_____

_____

_____

_____

12) Luke 9:23–24 speaks of the unflinching allegiance that Christ demands for all who would be His followers. How does the typical Christian experience measure up to this standard?

_____

_____

_____

_____

13) Describe the sacrifice Ruth made in choosing to accompany her mother-in-law and leave Moab. How can you imitate Ruth's love and selflessness in your own relationships with your in-laws or other family members?

_____

_____

_____

_____

Summing Up...

"When the Spirit empowers our lives and Christ is obeyed as the Lord of our hearts, our sins and weaknesses are dealt with and we find ourselves wanting to serve others, wanting to sacrifice for them and serve them—because

Christ's loving nature has truly become our own. Loving is the supernatural attitude of the Christian, because love is the nature of Christ. When a Christian does not love he has to do so intentionally and with effort—just as he must do to hold his breath. To become habitually unloving he must habitually resist Christ as the Lord of his heart. To continue the analogy to breathing, when Christ has His proper place in our hearts, we do not have to be told to love—just as we do not have to be told to breathe. Eventually it must happen, because loving is as natural to the spiritual person as breathing is to the natural person."—*John MacArthur*

Reflecting on the Text

14) What are some of the most painful choices you've made in your life? What specifically made the choices so difficult?

_____

_____

_____

_____

15) Why is doing what is best for others often very painful for us personally?

_____

_____

_____

_____

16) What specific attitudes or actions from the life of Ruth do you need to emulate today?

_____

_____

_____

_____

17) Rewrite Ruth 1:16–17 as an expression of your intended faithfulness to God.

_____

_____

Recording Your Thoughts

_____

_____

_____

_____

_____

_____

_____

_____

_____

_____

_____

_____

_____

_____

_____

_____

_____

_____

For further study, see the following passages:

Genesis 35:16	Genesis 38:11	Deuteronomy 25:5–6
Judges 21:25	2 Kings 3:27	Job 2:10
John 4:24	Romans 11	1 Thessalonians 1:9–10

Ruth's Devotion

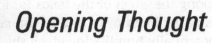

Opening Thought

1) What are the three kindest acts you've ever been the recipient of? How do you feel when someone showers you with undeserved or unexpected kindness?

_____

_____

_____

2) What do we mean when we say that someone is a gracious person?

_____

_____

3) What's the secret of developing a good reputation? How does someone improve a bad reputation?

_____

_____

_____

_____

Background of the Passage

After a ten-year sojourn in Moab, Naomi arrived back in Bethlehem accompanied by her daughter-in-law, Ruth. In a culture where widows were often forgotten and thus poverty-stricken, this unlikely twosome needed the basics of life. Fortunately for them, it was the time of the barley harvest. The younger Ruth volunteered to go out and glean along the edges of the fields for food. This was in keeping with the provisions of the Mosaic law and Jewish customs. But the plan was also risky and potentially humiliating given the low moral character of many of the reapers.

Chapter 2 reveals how God sovereignly and graciously directed Ruth to the field of Boaz, a close relative of Naomi. This prominent Bethlehemite noticed Ruth and not only provided for her and her mother-in-law, but also showed extra care and compassion for them. Boaz manifested the spirit of the law in going beyond what the Mosaic legislation required by feeding Ruth (2:14), letting Ruth glean among the sheaves (2:15), and leaving extra grain for her to glean (2:16).

Chapter 2 concludes with Naomi identifying Boaz as a kinsman-redeemer. Under Jewish law, a close relative could redeem (1) a family member sold into slavery (Leviticus 25:47–49); (2) land that needed to be sold under economic hardship (Leviticus 25:23–28); (3) the family name by virtue of a levirate marriage (Deuteronomy 25:5–10).

This custom pictures the reality of God the Redeemer doing a greater work (Psalm 19:14; Isaiah 41:14) by reclaiming those who needed to be spiritually redeemed out of slavery to sin (Psalm 107:2). Thus, Boaz pictures Christ, who as a Brother (Hebrews 2:17) redeemed those who were slaves to sin, had lost all earthly possessions/privilege in the fall, and had been alienated by sin from God. Boaz stands in the direct line of Christ (Matthew 1:5). This turn of events marks the point where Naomi's human emptiness (Ruth 1:21) begins to be refilled by the Lord. Her night of earthly doubt had been broken by the dawning of new hope.

Bible Passage

Read 2:1–23, noting the key words and definitions to the right of the passage.

¹ There was a relative of Naomi's husband, a man of great wealth, of the family of Elimelech. His name was Boaz.

² So Ruth the Moabitess said to Naomi, "Please let me go to the field, and glean heads of grain after him in whose sight I may find favor." And she said to her, "Go, my daughter."

³ Then she left, and went and gleaned in the field after the reapers. And she happened to come to the part of the field belonging to Boaz, who was of the family of Elimelech.

⁴ Now behold, Boaz came from Bethlehem, and said to the reapers, "The Lord be with you!" And they answered him, "The Lord bless you!"

⁵ Then Boaz said to his servant who was in charge of the reapers, "Whose young woman is this?"

⁶ So the servant who was in charge of the reapers answered and said, "It is the young Moabite woman who came back with Naomi from the country of Moab.

⁷ "And she said, 'Please let me glean and gather after the reapers among the sheaves.' So she came and has continued from morning until now, though she rested a little in the house."

⁸ Then Boaz said to Ruth, "You will listen, my daughter, will you not? Do not go to glean in another field, nor go from here, but stay close by my young women.

⁹ Let your eyes be on the field which they reap, and go after them. Have I not commanded the young men not to touch you? And when you are thirsty, go to the vessels and drink from what the young men have drawn."

¹⁰ So she fell on her face, bowed down to the ground, and said to him, "Why have I found favor in your eyes, that you should take notice of me, since I am a foreigner?"

¹¹ And Boaz answered and said to her, "It has been fully reported to me, all that you have done for

relative . . . of the family (v. 1)—possibly as close as a brother of Elimelech (see 4:3), but if not, certainly within the tribe or clan

a man of great wealth (v. 1)—literally "a man of valor" (see Judges 6:12) who had unusual capacity to obtain and protect his property

Boaz (v. 1)—His name means "in him is strength." He had never married or was a widower (see 1 Chronicles 2:11–12; Luke 3:32).

glean (v. 2)—Gleanings were stalks of grain left after the first cutting (see Ruth 2:3, 7, 8, 15, 17). These were dedicated to the needy, especially widows, orphans, and strangers. The Mosaic law commanded that the harvest should not be reaped to the corners nor the gleanings picked up.

she happened to come (v. 3) —Here is a classic example of God's providence at work.

part of the field (v. 3)—possibly a large community field in which Boaz had a plot

The Lord be with you (v. 4)—This unusual labor practice speaks to the exceptional godliness of Boaz and his workers.

sheaves (v. 15)—bundles of grain stalks tied together for transport to the threshing floor

morning . . . evening (vv. 7, 17)—Ruth proved to be diligent in her care for Naomi.

the house (v. 7)—most likely a temporary shelter built with branches by the side of the field (see 3:18)

my daughter (v. 8)—Boaz was about 45–55 years old as a contemporary of Elimelech and Naomi. He would naturally see Ruth as a

your mother-in-law since the death of your hus-
band, and how you have left your father and your
mother and the land of your birth, and have
come to a people whom you did not know before.

12 *The LORD repay your work, and a full reward be*
given you by the LORD God of Israel, under whose
wings you have come for refuge."

13 *Then she said, "Let me find favor in your sight,*
my lord; for you have comforted me, and have
spoken kindly to your maidservant, though I am
not like one of your maidservants."

14 *Now Boaz said to her at mealtime, "Come here,*
and eat of the bread, and dip your piece of bread
in the vinegar." So she sat beside the reapers, and
he passed parched grain to her; and she ate and
was satisfied, and kept some back.

15 *And when she rose up to glean, Boaz commanded*
his young men, saying, "Let her glean even
among the sheaves, and do not reproach her.

16 *Also let grain from the bundles fall purposely for*
her; leave it that she may glean, and do not
rebuke her."

17 *So she gleaned in the field until evening, and beat*
out what she had gleaned, and it was about an
ephah of barley.

18 *Then she took it up and went into the city, and*
her mother-in-law saw what she had gleaned. So
she brought out and gave to her what she had
kept back after she had been satisfied.

19 *And her mother-in-law said to her, "Where have*
you gleaned today? And where did you work?
Blessed be the one who took notice of you." So
she told her mother-in-law with whom she had
worked, and said, "The man's name with whom I
worked today is Boaz."

20 *Then Naomi said to her daughter-in-law,*
"Blessed be he of the LORD, who has not forsaken
His kindness to the living and the dead!" And
Naomi said to her, "This man is a relation of
ours, one of our close relatives."

daughter (3:10–11), much like Naomi did also (see 2:2, 22; 3:1, 16, 18). Boaz contrasted himself with younger men (3:10).

my young women (v. 8)—the ones who tied up the sheaves

young men (v. 9)—the ones who cut the grain with hand sickles (see 2:21)

a foreigner (v. 10)—Ruth remained ever mindful that she was an alien and as such must conduct herself humbly; she acknowledged the grace (literally, favor) of Boaz.

fully reported to me (v. 11)— This speaks to both Naomi's quickness to speak kindly of Ruth and Boaz's network of influence in Bethlehem. Ruth remained true to her promise (1:16–17).

wings . . . refuge (v. 12)— Scripture pictures God as catching Israel up on His wings in the Exodus (Exodus 19:4). God is here portrayed as a mother bird sheltering the young and fragile with her wings. Boaz blessed Ruth in light of her newfound commitment to and dependence on the Lord. Later, he would become God's answer to this prayer (see Ruth 3:9).

vinegar (v. 14)—sour wine mixed with a little oil used to quench thirst

among the sheaves (v. 15)— Boaz granted her request (2:7) to go beyond the law.

ephah (v. 17)—over one-half a bushel, weighing about thirty to forty pounds

what she had kept back (v. 18)—not the gleaned grain, but rather the lunch ration which Ruth did not eat (see 2:14)

His kindness (v. 20)—Naomi began to understand God's sovereign working, covenant loyalty,

21 *Ruth the Moabitess said, "He also said to me, 'You shall stay close by my young men until they have finished all my harvest.'"*

22 *And Naomi said to Ruth her daughter-in-law, "It is good, my daughter, that you go out with his young women, and that people do not meet you in any other field."*

23 *So she stayed close by the young women of Boaz, to glean until the end of barley harvest and wheat harvest; and she dwelt with her mother-in-law.*

loving kindness, and mercy toward her, because Ruth, without human direction (2:3), found the close relative Boaz.

one of our close relatives (v. 20)—The great kinsman-redeemer theme of Ruth begins here (see 3:9, 12; 4:1, 3, 6, 8, 14). A close relative could redeem a family member sold into slavery (Leviticus 25:47–49), land that needed to be sold under economic hardship (Leviticus 25:23–28), and the family name by virtue of a levirate marriage (Deuteronomy 25:5–10).

do not meet you (v. 22)—Ruth the Moabitess would not be treated with such mercy and grace by strangers outside of the family.

the end of . . . harvest (v. 23) —Barley harvest usually began about mid-April, and wheat harvest extended to mid-June—a period of intense labor for about two months. This generally coincided with the seven weeks between Passover and the Feast of Weeks, that is, Pentecost (see Leviticus 23:15–16).

Understanding the Text

4) What is gleaning? What risks or dangers does this chapter suggest that Ruth faced by performing this task?

_____

_____

_____

_____

_____

_____

_____

(verses to consider: Leviticus 19:9–10; Deuteronomy 24:19–21)

5) What was Ruth's reputation? How do you know?

_____

_____

_____

_____

_____

6) Boaz spoke a blessing on Ruth. What did it consist of?

_____

_____

_____

_____

_____

_____

(verses to consider: Psalms 17:8; 36:7; 57:1; 61:4; 63:7; 91:1, 4)

7) What are some of the specific acts of kindness that Boaz performed toward Ruth?

_____

_____

_____

_____

_____

_____

8) Naomi called Boaz "one of our kinsman-redeemers." What does this phrase mean?

_____

_____

_____

_____

_____

_____

Cross-Reference

Read Romans 6 and consider what it says about the redemption we have in Christ.

1 *What shall we say then? Shall we continue in sin that grace may abound?*

2 *Certainly not! How shall we who died to sin live any longer in it?*

3 *Or do you not know that as many of us as were baptized into Christ Jesus were baptized into His death?*

4 *Therefore we were buried with Him through baptism into death, that just as Christ was raised from the dead by the glory of the Father, even so we also should walk in newness of life.*

5 *For if we have been united together in the likeness of His death, certainly we also shall be in the likeness of His resurrection,*

6 *knowing this, that our old man was crucified with Him, that the body of sin might be done away with, that we should no longer be slaves of sin.*

7 *For he who has died has been freed from sin.*

8 *Now if we died with Christ, we believe that we shall also live with Him,*

9 *knowing that Christ, having been raised from the dead, dies no more. Death no longer has dominion over Him.*

10 *For the death that He died, He died to sin once for all; but the life that He lives, He lives to God.*

11 *Likewise you also, reckon yourselves to be dead indeed to sin, but alive to God in Christ Jesus our Lord.*

12 *Therefore do not let sin reign in your mortal body, that you should obey it in its lusts.*

13 *And do not present your members as instruments of unrighteousness to sin, but present yourselves to God as being alive from the dead, and your members as instruments of righteousness to God.*

14 *For sin shall not have dominion over you, for you are not under law but under grace.*

15 *What then? Shall we sin because we are not under law but under grace? Certainly not!*

16 *Do you not know that to whom you present yourselves slaves to obey, you are that one's slaves whom you obey, whether of sin leading to death, or of obedience leading to righteousness?*

17 *But God be thanked that though you were slaves of sin, yet you obeyed from the heart that form of doctrine to which you were delivered.*

18 *And having been set free from sin, you became slaves of righteousness.*

19 *I speak in human terms because of the weakness of your flesh. For just as you presented your members as slaves of uncleanness, and of lawlessness leading to more lawlessness, so now present your members as slaves of righteousness for holiness.*

20 *For when you were slaves of sin, you were free in regard to righteousness.*

21 *What fruit did you have then in the things of which you are now ashamed? For the end of those things is death.*

22 *But now having been set free from sin, and having become slaves of God, you have your fruit to holiness, and the end, everlasting life.*

23 *For the wages of sin is death, but the gift of God is eternal life in Christ Jesus our Lord.*

9) How does Boaz's treatment of Ruth as her kinsman-redeemer picture the later, greater work of Christ on behalf of sinners (as seen in Romans 6)?

_____

_____

_____

_____

_____

_____

(verses to consider: Matthew 20:28, 1 Corinthians 7:23; Galatians 3:13–14)

Exploring the Meaning

10) Galatians 5:22–23 speaks of the qualities that are evident in the life of one of who is God-inhabited. Which of these attributes do you see in Boaz (Ruth 2)? What about in Ruth?

_____

_____

_____

_____

_____

_____

_____

Summing Up...

"Sin is man's captor and slave owner, and it demands a price for his release. Death is the price that had to be paid for man's redemption from sin. Biblical redemption therefore refers to the act of God by which He Himself paid as a ransom the price for sin."—*John MacArthur*

Reflecting on the Text

11) Do you think Ruth and Naomi, upon arriving in Bethlehem, had any idea of all that God had in store for them? What does this tell us about God's plan for our lives? How should their experience encourage us to trust?

_____

_____

_____

_____

_____

_____

12) Why do you suppose Boaz demonstrated such kindness to Ruth?

_____

_____

_____

_____

13) List one or two things you could start doing or stop doing today to become a more faithful person.

_____

_____

_____

_____

_____

Recording Your Thoughts

_____

_____

_____

_____

_____

_____

_____

_____

_____

_____

_____

For further study, see the following passages:

Leviticus 23:22   Deuteronomy 16:9–12   Deuteronomy 23:3–4
Deuteronomy 32:11   Judges 11:1   Matthew 1:5
Luke 3:32   Romans 8:28–39

Ruth's Request

Opening Thought

1) If you are married, how did you meet your spouse?

_____

_____

_____

2) What are your favorite memories of when you two were dating? Who loved whom first? Where were you when you first said "I love you"?

_____

_____

_____

3) When did you become engaged? What were the circumstances?

_____

_____

_____

4) What is the most romantic proposal you've ever heard of?

_____

_____

_____

_____

25

Background of the Passage

This book tells a remarkable story of the sovereignty and goodness of God. In chapter one, we meet Naomi, a Jewish woman who fled to a neighboring land with her husband and two sons because of a famine in Israel. Ten years later we watch Naomi return to her homeland with a Moabite daughter-in-law named Ruth and not much else. As widows these women faced a bleak future. How would they survive in a culture built around intact families? More important, how would they make it in an increasingly decadent society (see Judges)?

The second chapter depicts how God graciously guided the young Moabitess, Ruth, to the field of Boaz. A prominent man of character, Boaz was also a close relative of Naomi. As such, he offered protection to Ruth as she gleaned in his fields among his reapers. He further provided generously for these women.

In chapter three, this delightful story of love, faithfulness, and devotion takes an unexpected turn. Encouraged by Ruth's positive experience in Boaz's field, Naomi instructed her in what she should do to ensure a brighter future. The mother-in-law told the daughter-in-law to put on her best appearance and to propose marriage to Boaz by utilizing an ancient Near Eastern custom. Since Boaz was a generation older than Ruth (2:8), this overture would indicate Ruth's desire to marry him which the older, gracious Boaz would not have initiated with a younger woman.

Ruth carefully followed Naomi's directions to solicit redemption by Boaz, while God prepared Boaz to redeem Ruth. Only one potential obstacle remained: a relative nearer than Boaz.

Bible Passage

Read 3:1–18, noting the key words and definitions to the right of the passage.

Ruth 3:1–18

1 Then Naomi her mother-in-law said to her, "My daughter, shall I not seek security for you, that it may be well with you?

2 Now Boaz, whose young women you were with, is

security (v. 1)—Naomi felt responsible, just as she did earlier (1:9), for Ruth's future husband and home.

tonight (v. 2)—Winnowing (tossing grain into the air to finish

he not our relative? In fact, he is winnowing barley tonight at the threshing floor.

³ Therefore wash yourself and anoint yourself, put on your best garment and go down to the threshing floor; but do not make yourself known to the man until he has finished eating and drinking.

⁴ Then it shall be, when he lies down, that you shall notice the place where he lies; and you shall go in, uncover his feet, and lie down; and he will tell you what you should do."

⁵ And she said to her, "All that you say to me I will do."

⁶ So she went down to the threshing floor and did according to all that her mother-in-law instructed her.

⁷ And after Boaz had eaten and drunk, and his heart was cheerful, he went to lie down at the end of the heap of grain; and she came softly, uncovered his feet, and lay down.

⁸ Now it happened at midnight that the man was startled, and turned himself; and there, a woman was lying at his feet.

⁹ And he said, "Who are you?" So she answered, "I am Ruth, your maidservant. Take your maidservant under your wing, for you are a close relative."

¹⁰ Then he said, "Blessed are you of the LORD, my daughter! For you have shown more kindness at the end than at the beginning, in that you did not go after young men, whether poor or rich.

¹¹ And now, my daughter, do not fear. I will do for you all that you request, for all the people of my town know that you are a virtuous woman.

¹² Now it is true that I am a close relative; however, there is a relative closer than I.

¹³ Stay this night, and in the morning it shall be that if he will perform the duty of a close relative for you—good; let him do it. But if he does not want to perform the duty for you, then I will perform the duty for you, as the LORD lives! Lie down until morning."

separating the grain from the chaff) normally occurred in late afternoon when the Mediterranean winds prevailed. Sifting and bagging the grain would have carried over past dark, and Boaz may have remained all night to guard the grain from theft.

threshing floor (v. 2)—usually a large hard area of earth or stone on the downwind (east) side of the village where threshing took place (loosening the grain from the straw and winnowing)

his heart was cheerful (v. 7) —Using the same language of 3:1 (security . . . be well), Boaz is described as having a sense of well-being which is most readily explained by the full harvest in contrast to previous years of famine.

Take your maidservant (v. 9) —Ruth righteously appealed to Boaz, using the language of Boaz's earlier prayer (2:12), to marry her according to the levirate custom.

kindness (v. 10)—Ruth's loyalty to Naomi, the Lord, and even Boaz is commended by Boaz.

after young men (v. 10)—Ruth demonstrated moral excellence in that she did not engage in immorality, she did not remarry outside the family, and she had appealed for levirate redemption to an older, godly man.

virtuous (v. 11)—In all respects Ruth personifies excellence (see Proverbs 31:10). This same language has been used of Boaz ("a man of great wealth" or more likely "a man of valor" in 2:1), thus making them the perfectly matched couple for an exemplary marriage.

a relative closer than I (v. 12) —Boaz righteously deferred to

14 *So she lay at his feet until morning, and she arose before one could recognize another. Then he said, "Do not let it be known that the woman came to the threshing floor."*

15 *Also he said, "Bring the shawl that is on you and hold it." And when she held it, he measured six ephahs of barley, and laid it on her. Then she went into the city.*

16 *So when she came to her mother-in-law, she said, "Is that you, my daughter?" Then she told her all that the man had done for her.*

17 *And she said, "These six ephahs of barley he gave me; for he said to me, 'Do not go empty-handed to your mother-in-law.'"*

18 *Then she said, "Sit still, my daughter, until you know how the matter will turn out; for the man will not rest until he has concluded the matter this day."*

someone else who was nearer in relationship to Elimelech. The nearer relative may have been Boaz's older brother (see 4:3), or Boaz may have been his cousin. The fact that the neighbor women said, "There is a son born to Naomi" at Obed's birth would suggest the brother or cousin relationship to Elimelech (4:17).

I will perform the duty (v. 13) —Boaz willingly accepted Ruth's proposal, if the nearer relative was unable or unwilling to exercise his levirate duty.

as the Lord lives (v. 13—the most solemn, binding oath a Jew could vow

lay at his feet (v. 14)— According to the text, no immorality occurred. Boaz even insisted on no appearance of evil.

six ephahs (v. 15)—The Hebrew text gives no standard of measurement; "ephah" has been inserted by the translators only as a possibility. However, six ephahs would weigh about two hundred pounds, which was far too much for Ruth to carry home in her shawl. Therefore, deemed most reasonable is six seahs (sixty to eighty pounds) which would have been twice the amount Ruth had previously gleaned (see 2:17).

this day (v. 18)—Naomi knew that Boaz was a man of integrity and would fulfill his promise with a sense of urgency. They needed to wait on the Lord to work through Boaz.

Understanding the Text

5) What did Naomi offer to do for Ruth (v. 1)? What instructions did she give? To what custom was she referring?

_____

_____

_____

(verses to consider: Leviticus 25:25–28; Deuteronomy 25:5–10)

6) How did Ruth respond to this seemingly strange advice from her mother-in-law? Does this surprise you?

_____

_____

_____

_____

7) What reasons might Ruth have given for not following such counsel?

_____

_____

_____

_____

(verses to consider: Proverbs 1:5; 11:14; 12:15; 27:9)

8) In what ways did Boaz demonstrate integrity and character in this night-time encounter with Ruth?

_____

_____

_____

Cross-Reference

Read the following passage from Proverbs 31 and compare its description to Ruth's character and behavior.

¹⁰ *Who can find a virtuous wife? For her worth is far above rubies.*
¹¹ *The heart of her husband safely trusts her; so he will have no lack of gain.*
¹² *She does him good and not evil all the days of her life.*
¹³ *She seeks wool and flax, and willingly works with her hands.*
¹⁴ *She is like the merchant ships, she brings her food from afar.*
¹⁵ *She also rises while it is yet night, and provides food for her household, and a portion for her maidservants.*
¹⁶ *She considers a field and buys it; from her profits she plants a vineyard.*
¹⁷ *She girds herself with strength, and strengthens her arms.*
¹⁸ *She perceives that her merchandise is good, and her lamp does not go out by night.*
¹⁹ *She stretches out her hands to the distaff, and her hand holds the spindle.*
²⁰ *She extends her hand to the poor, yes, she reaches out her hands to the needy.*
²¹ *She is not afraid of snow for her household, for all her household is clothed with scarlet.*
²² *She makes tapestry for herself; her clothing is fine linen and purple.*
²³ *Her husband is known in the gates, when he sits among the elders of the land.*
²⁴ *She makes linen garments and sells them, and supplies sashes for the merchants.*
²⁵ *Strength and honor are her clothing; she shall rejoice in time to come.*
²⁶ *She opens her mouth with wisdom, and on her tongue is the law of kindness.*
²⁷ *She watches over the ways of her household, and does not eat the bread of idleness.*
²⁸ *Her children rise up and call her blessed; her husband also, and he praises her:*
²⁹ *"Many daughters have done well, but you excel them all."*
³⁰ *Charm is deceitful and beauty is passing, but a woman who fears the LORD, she shall be praised.*
³¹ *Give her of the fruit of her hands, and let her own works praise her in the gates.*

9) Which of the descriptions in Proverbs 31 would apply to Ruth? Why?

_____

_____

_____

Exploring the Meaning

10) Based on what you've read and studied in the first three chapters of Ruth, what can you conclude about the relationship between this Jewish mother-in-law and her Moabite daughter-in-law?

_____

_____

_____

11) Read 1 Timothy 5:3–16. What does this passage say about widows? About relationships between older women and younger women?

_____

_____

_____

Ruth: The Proverbs 31 Wife

The "virtuous" wife of Proverbs 31:10 is personified by "virtuous" Ruth of whom the same Hebrew word is used (3:11). With amazing parallel, they share at least eight character traits (see below). One wonders (in concert with Jewish tradition) if King Lemuel's mother might not have been Bathsheba who orally passed the family heritage of Ruth's spotless reputation along to David's son Solomon. Lemuel, which means "devoted to God," could have been a family name for Solomon (see Jedediah, 2 Samuel 12:25), who then could have penned Proverbs 31:10–31 with Ruth in mind:

1. Devoted to her family (Ruth 1:15–18 // Proverbs 31:10–12, 23)
2. Delighted in her work (Ruth 2:2 // Proverbs 31:13)
3. Diligent in her labor (Ruth 2:7, 17, 23 // Proverbs 31:14–18,19–21, 24, 27)
4. Dedicated to godly speech (Ruth 2:10, 13 // Proverbs 13:26)
5. Dependent on God (Ruth 2:12 // Proverbs 31:25b, 30)
6. Dressed with care (Ruth 3:3 // Proverbs 31:22, 25a)
7. Discreet with men (Ruth 3:6–13 // Proverbs 31:11, 12, 23)
8. Delivered blessings (Ruth 4:14, 15 // Proverbs 31:28, 29, 31)

Summing Up...

"Life is made meaningful by relationships, the most meaningful of which is that between a husband and wife in marriage. Peter called it 'the grace of life' (1 Peter 3:7). Yet the fulfillment of that relationship is elusive. A marriage that continually gets better, richer, and more satisfying is rare today.

"From many voices today comes the claim that the very institution of marriage has failed to meet people's needs. But the fact is that it is not a matter of marriage having failed, since marriage has been increasingly avoided. Today, in place of exerting consistent effort and determination to fulfill the commitment it takes to make one's marriage work, the solution is to bail out."
—John MacArthur

Reflecting on the Text

12) What character qualities in Ruth or Boaz do you wish you possessed? What, with God's help, can you do to attain them?

_____

_____

_____

_____

13) If you are married, how would you rate your in-law relationships? What concrete steps could you take today to improve them?

_____

_____

_____

_____

14) It's not hard to see the sovereign hand of God at work behind the scenes in the lives of Ruth, Boaz, and Naomi. What are some events you've experienced that demonstrate God's grace and goodness?

Recording Your Thoughts

For further study, see the following passages:

Deuteronomy 25:5–10   Judges 18:20   1 Kings 21:7

Psalm 68:5   James 1:27

Ruth's Reward

Opening Thought

1) Most popular movies have a happy ending. What does this suggest about human nature?

_____

_____

_____

_____

2) How do you feel when you watch a film or read a novel that has a less-than-satisfying ending?

_____

_____

_____

_____

3) The phrase "and they lived happily ever after" is commonly used at the end of fairy tales. Does this phenomenon ever happen in real life? Why or why not?

_____

_____

_____

_____

Background of the Passage

During the dark time of the judges when Israel's future looked exceedingly grim, God quietly demonstrated His faithfulness to His wayward covenant people. He sovereignly orchestrated a series of events (a famine; the sudden, untimely deaths of three husbands; the surprising allegiance of a foreign daughter-in-law; and the rare kindness of a prosperous relative) to continue the family lineage through which the Messiah would one day come.

Chapter 1 details the return of the widows Naomi and Ruth from Moab to Bethlehem only to face an uncertain future. Chapter 2 documents Naomi's wise counsel and concern, Ruth's godly character, and Boaz's Christlike generosity. Chapter 3 is a record of Ruth's brave request that Boaz "redeem" her.

At last in chapter 4, we see God's divine plan fully blossom as Boaz redeems Naomi's land and Ruth's hand in marriage. Naomi, once empty (1:21), is full; Ruth, once a widow (1:5), is married; but most important, God has prepared Christ's line of descent in David, through Boaz and Obed, back to Judah (Genesis 49:10) to fulfill the proper Messianic lineage.

This book is a wonderful reminder that God's purposes cannot be thwarted. It is also a challenging picture of relationships marked by love and kindness.

Bible Passage

Read 4:1–22, noting the key words and definitions to the right of the passage.

Ruth 4:1–22

1 Now Boaz went up to the gate and sat down there; and behold, the close relative of whom Boaz had spoken came by. So Boaz said, "Come aside, friend, sit down here." So he came aside and sat down.

2 And he took ten men of the elders of the city, and said, "Sit down here." So they sat down.

3 Then he said to the close relative, "Naomi, who has come back from the country of Moab, sold the piece of land which belonged to our brother Elimelech.

went up (v. 1)—Apparently the threshing floor was below the level of the gate. Compare Ruth 3:3, "go down to the threshing floor."

the gate (v. 1)—the normal public place to transact business in ancient times (see 2 Samuel 15:2; Job 29:7)

friend (v. 1)—The Hebrew text is not clear whether Boaz called him directly by name (which is then not mentioned by the author) or indirectly.

⁴ *And I thought to inform you, saying, 'Buy it back in the presence of the inhabitants and the elders of my people. If you will redeem it, redeem it; but if you will not redeem it, then tell me, that I may know; for there is no one but you to redeem it, and I am next after you.'" And he said, "I will redeem it."*

⁵ *Then Boaz said, "On the day you buy the field from the hand of Naomi, you must also buy it from Ruth the Moabitess, the wife of the dead, to perpetuate the name of the dead through his inheritance."*

⁶ *And the close relative said, "I cannot redeem it for myself, lest I ruin my own inheritance. You redeem my right of redemption for yourself, for I cannot redeem it."*

⁷ *Now this was the custom in former times in Israel concerning redeeming and exchanging, to confirm anything: one man took off his sandal and gave it to the other, and this was a confirmation in Israel.*

⁸ *Therefore the close relative said to Boaz, "Buy it for yourself." So he took off his sandal.*

⁹ *And Boaz said to the elders and all the people, "You are witnesses this day that I have bought all that was Elimelech's, and all that was Chilion's and Mahlon's, from the hand of Naomi.*

¹⁰ *Moreover, Ruth the Moabitess, the widow of Mahlon, I have acquired as my wife, to perpetuate the name of the dead through his inheritance, that the name of the dead may not be cut off from among his brethren and from his position at the gate. You are witnesses this day."*

¹¹ *And all the people who were at the gate, and the elders, said, "We are witnesses. The LORD make the woman who is coming to your house like Rachel and Leah, the two who built the house of Israel; and may you prosper in Ephrathah and be famous in Bethlehem.*

¹² *May your house be like the house of Perez, whom*

ten men (v. 2)—This number apparently constituted a quorum to officially transact business, although only two or three witnesses were needed for judicial proceedings (see Deuteronomy 17:6).

Naomi . . . sold (v. 3)—this phrase could possibly be translated, "Naomi is about to sell." As a widow, she needed the money for living expenses, knowing that the land would ultimately be returned at Jubilee.

our brother Elimelech (v. 3)—Boaz and the unnamed relative were most likely either brothers or cousins.

Buy it back (v. 4)—as authorized by the Mosaic law (Leviticus 25:23–28)

you must also buy (v. 5)—Redeeming both Ruth and the land would not have been required by the letter of the levirate law (Deuteronomy 25:5–6). Perhaps this exemplified Boaz's desire to obey the spirit of the law, or maybe redemption of land and marriage had been combined by local tradition.

lest I ruin my own inheritance (v. 6)—He was unwilling to have the family portfolio split between his existing children and the potential offspring of a union with Ruth.

You redeem (v. 6)—The closer relative relinquished his legal right to the land and Ruth. This cleared the way for Boaz to redeem both.

took off his sandal (v. 7)—The writer explained to his own generation what had been a custom in former generations. This kind of tradition appears in Deuteronomy 25:5–10 and apparently continued at least to the time of Amos (see 2:6; 8:6). The

Tamar bore to Judah, because of the offspring which the LORD will give you from this young woman."

¹³ So Boaz took Ruth and she became his wife; and when he went in to her, the LORD gave her conception, and she bore a son.

¹⁴ Then the women said to Naomi, "Blessed be the LORD, who has not left you this day without a close relative; and may his name be famous in Israel!

¹⁵ And may he be to you a restorer of life and a nourisher of your old age; for your daughter-in-law, who loves you, who is better to you than seven sons, has borne him."

¹⁶ Then Naomi took the child and laid him on her bosom, and became a nurse to him.

¹⁷ Also the neighbor women gave him a name, saying, "There is a son born to Naomi." And they called his name Obed. He is the father of Jesse, the father of David.

¹⁸ Now this is the genealogy of Perez: Perez begot Hezron;

¹⁹ Hezron begot Ram, and Ram begot Amminadab;

²⁰ Amminadab begot Nahshon, and Nahshon begot Salmon;

²¹ Salmon begot Boaz, and Boaz begot Obed;

²² Obed begot Jesse, and Jesse begot David.

closer relative legally transferred his right to the property as symbolized by the sandal, most likely that of the nearer relative.

I have bought (v. 9)—Boaz exercised his legal option to redeem both the land and Ruth before appropriate witnesses.

the widow of Mahlon (v. 10) —Only here is Ruth's former husband identified (see 1:5 note). Therefore, it can also be assumed that Chilion married Orpah.

I have acquired as my wife (v. 10)—Boaz exercised the spirit of the law and became Ruth's kinsman-redeemer (Deuteronomy 25:5–6).

the name of the dead (v. 10) —Perpetuation of the family name (1 Samuel 24:21) was an important feature that the levirate process provided (see Deuteronomy 25:6).

We are witnesses (v. 11)— This affirmation signaled the strong approval of the city.

like Rachel and Leah (v. 11)— Rachel, the most beloved wife of Jacob, was buried nearby (Genesis 35:19); Leah was the mother of Judah (by Jacob) their namesake descendant (Genesis 29:35). This remembrance went back almost nine hundred years to 1915 B.C.

Perez . . . Tamar . . . Judah (v. 12)—Tamar, the widow of Judah's first son Er, when denied a levirate marriage to Judah's remaining son Shelah (38:14), took matters into her own hands and immorally consorted with her father-in-law Judah (38:18). Perez, the firstborn of twins by Tamar, became the main ancestor of the Ephrathites and Bethlehemites (1 Chronicles 2:3–5, 19, 50–51; 4:4).

offspring (v. 12)—The firstborn son would be considered the son of Mahlon. Additional sons would legally be the offspring of Boaz (Deuteronomy 25:6).

he went in to her (v. 13)—Old Testament euphemism for sexual intercourse

the LORD gave her conception (v. 13)—as with Rachel (Genesis 30:22) and Leah (Genesis 29:31), so also with Ruth

the LORD . . . has not left you (v. 14)—in contrast to Naomi's worst moments of despair (Ruth 1:20–21)

a close relative . . . his name (v. 14)—refers to Obed, not Boaz (see 4:11), who cared for Naomi in her latter years

better . . . than seven sons (v. 15)—Seven represented the number of perfection and thus seven sons would make the complete family (see 1 Samuel 2:5). However, Ruth exceeded this standard all by herself.

a nurse to him (v. 16)—This expresses the natural affection of a godly grandmother for her God-given grandson.

the neighbor women gave him a name (v. 17)—This is the only place in the Old Testament where a child was named by someone other than the immediate family.

a son born to Naomi (v. 17)—Ruth vicariously bore the son that would restore the family name of Naomi's deceased son Mahlon (see 4:1).

Obed . . . Jesse . . . David (v. 17)—this complete genealogy appears identically in four other biblical texts (Ruth 4:21, 22; 1 Chronicles 2:12–15; Matthew 1:5, 6; Luke 3:31–32). Boaz and Ruth were the great-grandparents of David.

Perez . . . David (vv. 18–22)—This representative genealogy, which spans nine centuries from Perez (1885 B.C.) to David (1040 B.C.), specifically names ten generations. The first five (Perez to Nahshon) cover the Patriarchal times to the Exodus and wilderness wanderings. Salmon to David covers Joshua's lifetime and the judges to the monarchy. This genealogical compression by omission does not signal faulty records, because in Jewish thinking "son" could mean "descendant" (see Matthew 1:1). The purpose of a family record was not necessarily to include every generation but, rather, to establish incontestable succession by way of the more notable ancestors.

Salmon begot Boaz (v. 21)—Since Matthew 1:5 lists Rahab the harlot, who lived 1425–1350 B.C., as Salmon's wife, it thus indicates that some generations have been selectively omitted between Salmon and Boaz (1160–1090 B.C.).

David (v. 22)—Looking back at Ruth from a New Testament perspective, latent Messianic implications become more apparent (see Matthew 1:1). The fruit that is promised later on in the Davidic Covenant finds its seedbed here. The hope of a Messianic king and kingdom (2 Samuel 7:12–14) will be fulfilled in the Lord Jesus Christ (Revelation 19–20) through the lineage of David's grandfather Obed, who was born to Boaz and Ruth the Moabitess.

Understanding the Text

4) Why did Boaz go to the city gate, and what laws or customs was he following?

_____

_____

_____

_____

(verses to consider: Genesis 38:8; Matthew 22:23–28)

5) Since Boaz lived at a time when "everyone did what was right in his own eyes" (Judges 21:25), why do you think he was so eager to follow the Mosaic law?

_____

_____

_____

_____

6) What was the initial response of the unnamed "close relative" whom Boaz approached? What prompted him to change his mind?

_____

_____

_____

_____

7) What was the significance of taking off one's sandal as part of a legal transaction?

_____

_____

_____

_____

(verses to consider Deuteronomy 25:5–10; Amos 2:6)

8) Why did the author include a genealogy at the end of chapter 4?

_____

_____

_____

Cross-Reference

Read 2 Samuel 7:1–17.

1 *Now it came to pass when the king was dwelling in his house, and the LORD had given him rest from all his enemies all around,*

2 *that the king said to Nathan the prophet, "See now, I dwell in a house of cedar, but the ark of God dwells inside tent curtains."*

3 *Then Nathan said to the king, "Go, do all that is in your heart, for the LORD is with you."*

4 *But it happened that night that the word of the LORD came to Nathan, saying,*

5 *"Go and tell My servant David, 'Thus says the LORD: "Would you build a house for Me to dwell in?*

6 *For I have not dwelt in a house since the time that I brought the children of Israel up from Egypt, even to this day, but have moved about in a tent and in a tabernacle.*

7 *Wherever I have moved about with all the children of Israel, have I ever spoken a word to anyone from the tribes of Israel, whom I commanded to shepherd My people Israel, saying, 'Why have you not built Me a house of cedar?'*

8 *Now therefore, thus shall you say to My servant David, 'Thus says the LORD of hosts: "I took you from the sheepfold, from following the sheep, to be ruler over My people, over Israel.*

9 *And I have been with you wherever you have gone, and have cut off all your enemies from before you, and have made you a great name, like the name of the great men who are on the earth.*

10 *Moreover I will appoint a place for My people Israel, and will plant them, that they may dwell in a place of their own and move no more; nor shall the sons of wickedness oppress them anymore, as previously,*

11 *since the time that I commanded judges to be over My people Israel, and have caused you to rest from all your enemies. Also the LORD tells you that He will make you a house.*

12 *When your days are fulfilled and you rest with your fathers, I will set up your*

seed after you, who will come from your body, and I will establish his kingdom.
13 *He shall build a house for My name, and I will establish the throne of his king-dom forever.*
14 *I will be his Father, and he shall be My son. If he commits iniquity, I will chas-ten him with the rod of men and with the blows of the sons of men.*
15 *But My mercy shall not depart from him, as I took it from Saul, whom I removed from before you.*
16 *And your house and your kingdom shall be established forever before you. Your throne shall be established forever."*
17 *According to all these words and according to all this vision, so Nathan spoke to David.*

9) What does the story of Ruth (and her giving birth to Obed) have to do with the covenant God made with David?

_____

_____

_____

_____

Exploring the Meaning

10) Read Matthew 1:5. Why is it significant that Rahab the non-Jewish harlot and Ruth the Moabitess were part of Messiah's lineage?

_____

_____

_____

_____

11) Ruth was just an obscure Moabite girl when God chose her to be part of His plan. David was just an unknown shepherd boy when God chose him to be part of His plan. What does this say about the kind of people God uses?

_____

_____

_____

_____

Summing Up...

"History belongs to God, not to the puny plans of man or the perverse power of Satan. History is written and directed by its Creator, who will see it through to the fulfillment of His own ultimate purpose—the summing up of all things in Christ. He designed His great plan in the ages past; He now sovereignly works it out according to His divine will; and in the fullness of the times He will complete and perfect it in His Son, in whom it will forever operate in righteous harmony and glorious newness along with all things in the heavens and things upon the earth."—*John MacArthur*

Reflecting on the Text

12) Think back over Ruth's life and note the crucial turning points. How would her life have been different had she made choices other than the ones she made?

_____

_____

_____

_____

13) What five adjectives would you use to describe Boaz? What about Ruth?

_____

_____

_____

14) Which of those qualities are present in your life? Which ones would you like to be present? What would it take to develop those qualities?

_____

_____

_____

_____

_____

Recording Your Thoughts

_____

_____

_____

_____

_____

_____

_____

_____

_____

_____

_____

_____

_____

_____

_____

_____

_____

_____

For further study, see the following passages:

Genesis 38:1–30   Leviticus 25:28   Deuteronomy 19:15
Psalm 127:3   Jeremiah 32:6–15   Lamentations 5:14
Amos 8:6

THE BOOK OF ESTHER

Introduction

"Esther" has served as the title without variation through the ages. This book and the Book of Ruth are the only Old Testament books named after women. The New Testament does not quote or allude to Esther (or Song of Solomon, Obadiah, and Nahum).

Hadassah (2:7), meaning "myrtle," was the Hebrew name of Esther, which came either from the Persian word "star" or possibly from the name of the Babylonian love goddess, Ishtar. As the orphaned daughter of her father Abihail, Esther grew up in Persia with her older cousin, Mordecai, who raised her as if she were his own daughter (2:7, 15).

Author and Date

The author remains unknown, although Mordecai, Ezra, and Nehemiah have been suggested. Whoever penned Esther possessed a detailed knowledge of Persian customs, etiquette, and history, plus particular familiarity with the palace at Shushan (1:5–7). The author also exhibited intimate knowledge of the Hebrew calendar and customs, while additionally showing a strong sense of Jewish nationalism. Possibly a Persian Jew, who later moved back to Israel, wrote Esther.

This is the seventeenth book in the literary chronology of the Old Testament and closes the Old Testament historical section. Only Ezra 7–10, Nehemiah, and Malachi report later Old Testament history than Esther. The account in Esther ends in 473 B.C. before Ahasuerus died by assassination (465 B.C.). Esther 10:2 speaks as though Ahasuerus's reign has been completed, so the earliest possible writing date would be after his reign around the mid-fifth century B.C. The latest reasonable date would be prior to 331 B.C., when Greece conquered Persia.

Background and Setting

The events recorded in this book occurred during the Persian period of world history, 539 B.C. (Daniel 5:30–31) to 331 B.C. (Daniel 8:1–27). Ahasuerus ruled from 486 to 465 B.C.; Esther covers the 483–473 B.C. portion of his reign. The name Ahasuerus represents the Hebrew transliteration of the Persian name "Khshayarsha," while "Xerxes" represents his Greek name.

These events occurred during the wider time span between the first return of the Jews after the seventy year captivity in Babylon (Daniel 9:1–19) under Zerubbabel (538 B.C., Ezra 1–6) and the second return led by Ezra (458 B.C., Ezra 7–10). Nehemiah's journey (the third return) from Susa to Jerusalem (Nehemiah 1–2) occurred later (445 B.C.).

Esther and Exodus both chronicle how vigorously foreign powers tried to eliminate the Jewish race and how God sovereignly preserved His people in accordance with His covenant promise to Abraham of around 2100–2075 B.C. (Genesis 12:1–3; 17:1–8). As a result of God's prevailing, Esther 9–10 records the beginning of Purim—a new annual festival in the twelfth month (February–March) to celebrate the nation's survival. Purim became one of two festivals given outside of the Mosaic legislation that are still celebrated by Jews. Hanukkah, or the Festival of Lights, is the other (see John 10:22).

Historical and Theological Themes

All 167 verses of Esther have ultimately been accepted as canonical, although the absence of God's name anywhere has caused some to unnecessarily doubt its authenticity. The Greek Septuagint (LXX) added an extra 107 apocryphal verses that supposedly compensated for this lack. Along with Song of Solomon, Ruth, Ecclesiastes, and Lamentations, Esther stands with the Old Testament books of the Megilloth, or "five scrolls." Rabbis read these books in the synagogue on five special occasions during the year—Esther being read at Purim (see Esther 9:20–32).

The historical genesis for the drama played out between Mordecai (a Benjamite descendant of Saul—2:5) and Haman (an Agagite—3:1, 10; 8:3, 5; 9:24) goes back almost a thousand years when the Jews exited from Egypt (1445 B.C.) and were attacked by the Amalekites (Exodus 17:8–16), whose lineage began with Amalek, son of Esau (Genesis 36:12). God pronounced His curse on the Amalekites, which resulted in their total elimination as a people (Exodus 17:14; Deuteronomy 25:17–19). Although Saul (1030 B.C.) received orders to kill all the Amalekites, including their king Agag (1 Samuel 15:2–3), he disobeyed (15:7–9) and incurred God's displeasure (15:11, 26; 28:18). Samuel finally hacked Agag into pieces (15:32, 33). Because of his lineage from Agag, Haman carried deep hostility toward the Jews.

The time of Esther arrived 550 years after the death of Agag, but despite such passage of time, neither Haman the Agagite nor Mordecai the Benjamite had forgotten the tribal feud that still smoldered in their souls. This explains why Mordecai refused to bow down to Haman (3:2, 3) and why Haman so viciously attempted to exterminate the Jewish race (3:5, 6, 13). As expected, God's prophecy to extinguish the Amalekites (Exodus 17:14; Deuteronomy 25:17–19) and God's promise to preserve the Jews (Genesis 17:1–8) prevailed.

Because of God's faithfulness to save His people, the festival of Purim (named after the Akkadian word for "lot"—Esther 3:7; 9:26), an annual, two-day holiday of feasting, rejoicing, sending food to one another, and giving gifts to the poor (9:21–22), was decreed to be celebrated in every generation, by every family, in every province and city (9:27–28). Esther later added a new feature of fasting with lamentation (9:31). Purim is not mentioned in the Bible again, although it has been celebrated throughout the centuries by the Jewish people.

Esther could be compared to a chess game. God and Satan (as invisible players) moved real kings, queens, and nobles. When Satan put Haman into place, it was as if he announced "Check!" God then positioned Esther and Mordecai in order to put Satan into "Checkmate!" Ever since the Fall (Genesis 3:1–19), Satan has attempted to spiritually sever God's relationship with His human creation and disrupt God's covenant promises with Israel. For example, Christ's line through the tribe of Judah had been murderously reduced to Joash alone, who was rescued and preserved (2 Chronicles 22:10–12). Later, Herod slaughtered the infants of Bethlehem, thinking Christ was among them (Matthew 2:16). Satan tempted Christ to denounce God and worship him (Matthew 4:9). Peter, at Satan's insistence, tried to block Christ's journey to Calvary (Matthew 16:22). Finally, Satan entered into Judas, who then betrayed Christ to the Jews and Romans (Luke 22:3–6). While God is not mentioned in Esther, He is everywhere apparent as the One who opposed and foiled Satan's diabolical schemes by providential intervention.

In Esther, all of God's unconditional covenant promises to Abraham (Genesis 17:1–8) and to David (2 Samuel 7:8–16) were jeopardized. However, God's love for Israel is nowhere more apparent than in this dramatic rescue of His people from pending elimination. "Behold, He who keeps Israel shall neither slumber nor sleep" (Psalm 121:4).

Intrepretive Challenges

The most obvious question raised by the Book of Esther comes from the fact that God, as in Song of Solomon, is nowhere mentioned. Nor does the writer or any participant refer to the law of God, the Levitical sacrifices, worship, or prayer. The skeptic might ask, "Why would God never be mentioned when the Persian king receives over 175 references? Since God's sovereignty prevailed to save the Jews, why does He then not receive appropriate recognition?"

It seems satisfying to respond that if God desired to be mentioned, He could just as sovereignly have moved the author to write of Him as He acted to save Israel. This situation seems to be more of a problem at the human level than the divine because Esther is the classic illustration of God's providence as He, the unseen power, controls everything for His purpose. The book records no miracles either, but the preservation of Israel through providential control of every event and person reveals the omniscience and omnipotence of Jehovah. Whether God is named is not the issue. He is clearly the main character in the drama.

Second, why were Mordecai and Esther so secular in their lifestyles? Esther (2:6–20) does not seem to have the zeal for holiness like Daniel (Daniel 1:8–20). Mordecai kept his and Esther's Jewish heritage secret, unlike Daniel (Daniel 6:5). The law of God was absent in contrast to Ezra (Ezra 7:10). Nehemiah had a heart for Jerusalem that seemingly eluded the affections of Esther and Mordecai (Nehemiah 1:1—2:5).

The following observations help to shed some light on these issues. First, this short book does not record everything. Perhaps Mordecai and Esther actually possessed a deeper faith than becomes apparent here (see Esther 4:16). Second, even godly Nehemiah did not mention his God when talking to King Artaxerxes (Nehemiah 2:1–8). Third, the Jewish festivals which provided structure for worship had been lost long before Esther—for example, Passover (2 Kings 23:22) and Pentecost (Nehemiah 8:17). Fourth, possibly the anti-Jewish letter written by the Samaritans to Ahasuerus several years earlier had frightened them (486 B.C., Ezra 4:6). Fifth, the evil intentions of Haman did not just first surface when Mordecai refused to bow down (Esther 3:1, 2). Most likely they were long before shared by others which would have intimidated the Jewish population. Sixth, Esther did identify with her Jewish heritage at a most appropriate time (7:3–4). Yet, the nagging question of why Esther and Mordecai did not seem to have the same kind of open devotion to God as did Daniel remains. Further, Nehemiah's prayer (Nehemiah 1:5–11, especially verse 7) seems to indicate a spiritual lethargy among the Jewish exiles in Susa. So this issue must ultimately be resolved by God since He alone knows human hearts.

Additional Notes:

Esther's Ascension

Opening Thought

1) What's the most nerve-wracking, suspenseful story you've ever read or seen on film? What made it so compelling?

_____

_____

_____

2) What do you think it would be like to be the ruler of an entire nation or empire? What would you do if you were declared the "benevolent dictator" of this country?

_____

_____

_____

3) What is your opinion of beauty contests? Of those who partici-pate in them? Why?

_____

_____

_____

_____

Background of the Passage

The Old Testament books of Ezra and Nehemiah tell the story of the Jews who returned to the land of promise following their seventy-year God-ordained captivity. This book, on the other hand, reveals what happened to the remnant of Jews who elected to remain in Persia.

It has been noted that the name of God does not appear even once in the ten chapters of Esther. Nevertheless God's fingerprints are all over the book. The Lord used a beautiful young Jewish girl and her wise uncle to thwart a genocidal plot in a dramatic story filled with suspense, intrigue, and surprises. This great deliverance of the Jews was, and is, commemorated by the Feast of Purim, an annual celebration of God's faithfulness to His people.

Esther's rise to a position of influence began in Susa when King Ahasuerus ordered his wife, Queen Vashti, to show off her beauty at a large and lavish banquet (chapter 1). After Vashti balked at this edict, the king was counseled to find a new queen (lest other women in the empire become emboldened to defy their husbands).

Esther, her Jewish ancestry a secret, became a contestant in this royal beauty contest (chapter 2) to find a new queen. The result was that "the king loved Esther more than all the other women, and she obtained grace and favor in his sight more than all the virgins; so he set the royal crown upon her head and made her queen instead of Vashti" (2:17).

Bible Passage

Read 1:1—2:20, noting the key words and definitions to the right of the passage.

Esther 1:1—2:20

¹ Now it came to pass in the days of Ahasuerus (this was the Ahasuerus who reigned over one hundred and twenty-seven provinces, from India to Ethiopia),

² in those days when King Ahasuerus sat on the throne of his kingdom, which was in Shushan the citadel,

one hundred and twenty-seven provinces (v. 1)—The kingdom comprised twenty regions (3:12; 8:9; 9:3) which were further divided into provinces ruled over by governors (3:12).

India to Ethiopia (v. 1)—Ethiopia, not Asia Minor, is mentioned as representing the western edge of the kingdom to avoid any remembrance of the king's

³ that in the third year of his reign he made a feast for all his officials and servants—the powers of Persia and Media, the nobles, and the princes of the provinces being before him—

⁴ when he showed the riches of his glorious kingdom and the splendor of his excellent majesty for many days, one hundred and eighty days in all.

⁵ And when these days were completed, the king made a feast lasting seven days for all the people who were present in Shushan the citadel, from great to small, in the court of the garden of the king's palace.

⁶ There were white and blue linen curtains fastened with cords of fine linen and purple on silver rods and marble pillars; and the couches were of gold and silver on a mosaic pavement of alabaster, turquoise, and white and black marble.

⁷ And they served drinks in golden vessels, each vessel being different from the other, with royal wine in abundance, according to the generosity of the king.

⁸ In accordance with the law, the drinking was not compulsory; for so the king had ordered all the officers of his household, that they should do according to each man's pleasure.

⁹ Queen Vashti also made a feast for the women in the royal palace which belonged to King Ahasuerus.

¹⁰ On the seventh day, when the heart of the king was merry with wine, he commanded Mehuman, Biztha, Harbona, Bigtha, Abagtha, Zethar, and Carcas, seven eunuchs who served in the presence of King Ahasuerus,

¹¹ to bring Queen Vashti before the king, wearing her royal crown, in order to show her beauty to the people and the officials, for she was beautiful to behold.

¹² But Queen Vashti refused to come at the king's command brought by his eunuchs; therefore the king was furious, and his anger burned within him.

previous defeat by the Greeks (481–479 B.C., see 8:9). This description also avoided any confusion with the Ahasuerus of Daniel 9:1.

Shushan the citadel (v. 2)—Shushan (the Hebrew rendering of the Greek Susa), the winter residence, was one of four capital cities; the other three included Babylon, Ecbatana (Ezra 6:2), and Persepolis. The citadel refers to the fortified palace complex built above the city for protection.

the third year (v. 3)—483 B.C. This probably included the planning phase for Ahasuerus's later campaign against Greece in which the king suffered a humiliating defeat (481–479 B.C.).

Persia and Media (v. 4)—Cyrus the Persian inherited Media, and thus the name Media became just as prominent as Persia (550 B.C.).

Queen Vashti (v. 9)—Greek literature records her name as Amestris. She gave birth (483 B.C.) to Ahasuerus's third son, Artaxerxes, who later succeeded his father Ahasuerus on the throne.

Vashti refused (v. 12)—Her reason is not recorded, although suggestions have included that her appearance would have involved lewd behavior before drunken men, or that she was still pregnant with Artaxerxes.

13 Then the king said to the wise men who understood the times (for this was the king's manner toward all who knew law and justice,

14 those closest to him being Carshena, Shethar, Admatha, Tarshish, Meres, Marsena, and Memucan, the seven princes of Persia and Media, who had access to the king's presence, and who ranked highest in the kingdom):

15 "What shall we do to Queen Vashti, according to law, because she did not obey the command of King Ahasuerus brought to her by the eunuchs?"

16 And Memucan answered before the king and the princes: "Queen Vashti has not only wronged the king, but also all the princes, and all the people who are in all the provinces of King Ahasuerus.

17 For the queen's behavior will become known to all women, so that they will despise their husbands in their eyes, when they report, 'King Ahasuerus commanded Queen Vashti to be brought in before him, but she did not come.'

18 This very day the noble ladies of Persia and Media will say to all the king's officials that they have heard of the behavior of the queen. Thus there will be excessive contempt and wrath.

19 If it pleases the king, let a royal decree go out from him, and let it be recorded in the laws of the Persians and the Medes, so that it will not be altered, that Vashti shall come no more before King Ahasuerus; and let the king give her royal position to another who is better than she.

20 When the king's decree which he will make is proclaimed throughout all his empire (for it is great), all wives will honor their husbands, both great and small."

21 And the reply pleased the king and the princes, and the king did according to the word of Memucan.

22 Then he sent letters to all the king's provinces, to each province in its own script, and to every people in their own language, that each man

the seven princes (v. 14)—These highest ranking officials (see Ezra 7:14) were perhaps equivalent to the magi of Daniel 1:20.

will not be altered (v. 19)—The irrevocable nature of Persian law played an important role in how the rest of Esther concluded (see 8:8).

letters (v. 22)—The efficient Persian communication network (a rapid relay by horses) played an important role in speedily publishing kingdom edicts (see 3:12–14; 8:9–10, 14; 9:20, 30).

should be master in his own house, and speak in the language of his own people.

2:1 After these things, when the wrath of King Ahasuerus subsided, he remembered Vashti, what she had done, and what had been decreed against her.

2 Then the king's servants who attended him said: "Let beautiful young virgins be sought for the king;

3 and let the king appoint officers in all the provinces of his kingdom, that they may gather all the beautiful young virgins to Shushan the citadel, into the women's quarters, under the custody of Hegai the king's eunuch, custodian of the women. And let beauty preparations be given them.

4 Then let the young woman who pleases the king be queen instead of Vashti." This thing pleased the king, and he did so.

5 In Shushan the citadel there was a certain Jew whose name was Mordecai the son of Jair, the son of Shimei, the son of Kish, a Benjamite.

6 Kish had been carried away from Jerusalem with the captives who had been captured with Jeconiah king of Judah, whom Nebuchadnezzar the king of Babylon had carried away.

7 And Mordecai had brought up Hadassah, that is, Esther, his uncle's daughter, for she had neither father nor mother. The young woman was lovely and beautiful. When her father and mother died, Mordecai took her as his own daughter.

8 So it was, when the king's command and decree were heard, and when many young women were gathered at Shushan the citadel, under the custody of Hegai, that Esther also was taken to the king's palace, into the care of Hegai the custodian of the women.

9 Now the young woman pleased him, and she obtained his favor; so he readily gave beauty

After these things (2:1)—most likely during the latter portion of the king's ill-fated war with Greece (481–479 B.C.)

he remembered Vashti (v. 1) —The king was legally unable to restore Vashti (see 1:19–22), so the counselors proposed a new plan with promise.

Mordecai (v. 5)—among the fourth generation of deported Jews

Kish (v. 5)—Mordecai's great-grandfather, who actually experienced the Babylonian deportation; after Babylon fell to Medo-Persia (539 B.C.), Jews were moved to other parts of the new kingdom; Kish represents a Benjamite family name that could be traced back (to about 1100 B.C.) to Saul's father

Jeconiah (v. 6)—former king of Judah (also known as Jehoiachin and Coniah) who was deported (597 B.C.); due to his disobedience, the Lord removed his descendants from the line of David to Christ

Esther also was taken (v. 8)— It is impossible to tell if Esther went voluntarily or against her will.

pleased him (v. 9)—That she pleased Hegai points to God's providential control.

preparations to her, besides her allowance. Then seven choice maidservants were provided for her from the king's palace, and he moved her and her maidservants to the best place in the house of the women.

10 Esther had not revealed her people or family, for Mordecai had charged her not to reveal it.

11 And every day Mordecai paced in front of the court of the women's quarters, to learn of Esther's welfare and what was happening to her.

12 Each young woman's turn came to go in to King Ahasuerus after she had completed twelve months' preparation, according to the regulations for the women, for thus were the days of their preparation apportioned: six months with oil of myrrh, and six months with perfumes and preparations for beautifying women.

13 Thus prepared, each young woman went to the king, and she was given whatever she desired to take with her from the women's quarters to the king's palace.

14 In the evening she went, and in the morning she returned to the second house of the women, to the custody of Shaashgaz, the king's eunuch who kept the concubines. She would not go in to the king again unless the king delighted in her and called for her by name.

15 Now when the turn came for Esther the daughter of Abihail the uncle of Mordecai, who had taken her as his daughter, to go in to the king, she requested nothing but what Hegai the king's eunuch, the custodian of the women, advised. And Esther obtained favor in the sight of all who saw her.

16 So Esther was taken to King Ahasuerus, into his royal palace, in the tenth month, which is the month of Tebeth, in the seventh year of his reign.

17 The king loved Esther more than all the other women, and she obtained grace and favor in his sight more than all the virgins; so he set the royal

not to reveal it (v. 10)—possibly because of the hostile letter mentioned in Ezra 4:6 or the anti-Semitic sentiments of Haman and other like-minded people

the second house (v. 14)—the place of concubines

obtained favor (v. 15)—according to the Lord's providential plan

Tebeth (v. 16)—the tenth month, corresponding to December–January

the seventh year (v. 16)—479–478 B.C.; four years had elapsed since Vashti's fall from favor.

crown upon her head and made her queen instead of Vashti.

¹⁸ Then the king made a great feast, the Feast of Esther, for all his officials and servants; and he proclaimed a holiday in the provinces and gave gifts according to the generosity of a king.

¹⁹ When virgins were gathered together a second time, Mordecai sat within the king's gate.

²⁰ Now Esther had not revealed her family and her people, just as Mordecai had charged her, for Esther obeyed the command of Mordecai as when she was brought up by him.

a holiday (v. 18)—This probably refers to a remission of taxes or release from military service.

a second time (v. 19)—Perhaps the king intended to add some more girls to his concubine collection.

Understanding the Text

4) How would you describe the feast given by Ahasuerus? What does this extravagant affair say about him—his character, his rule, his values?

_____

_____

_____

5) Why did Vashti refuse to comply with the king's wishes? Who was right? Why?

_____

_____

_____

6) What was the king's motive for deposing Vashti?

_____

_____

_____

7) What does the above passage reveal about Esther? About her relationship with Mordecai?

_____

_____

_____

Cross-Reference

Read Jeremiah 24:1–7.

¹ *The LORD showed me, and there were two baskets of figs set before the temple of the LORD, after Nebuchadnezzar king of Babylon had carried away captive Jeconiah the son of Jehoiakim, king of Judah, and the princes of Judah with the craftsmen and smiths, from Jerusalem, and had brought them to Babylon.*

² *One basket had very good figs, like the figs that are first ripe; and the other basket had very bad figs which could not be eaten, they were so bad.*

³ *Then the LORD said to me, "What do you see, Jeremiah?" And I said, "Figs, the good figs, very good; and the bad, very bad, which cannot be eaten, they are so bad."*

⁴ *Again the word of the LORD came to me, saying,*

⁵ *"Thus says the LORD, the God of Israel: 'Like these good figs, so will I acknowledge those who are carried away captive from Judah, whom I have sent out of this place for their own good, into the land of the Chaldeans.*

⁶ *For I will set My eyes on them for good, and I will bring them back to this land; I will build them and not pull them down, and I will plant them and not pluck them up.*

⁷ *Then I will give them a heart to know Me, that I am the LORD; and they shall be My people, and I will be their God, for they shall return to Me with their whole heart.'"*

8) What do the good figs represent in Jeremiah's vision above? What about the bad figs? Into which category would you put the family of Mordecai and Esther?

_____

_____

_____

9) What does this passage (together with Esther 1 and 2) say about God's sovereignty—that is, His control of both personal affairs and international situations?

_____

_____

_____

Exploring the Meaning

10) Read Jeremiah 22:24–30. What does this passage say about Jeconiah? What is the connection between Mordecai and Jeconiah (see Esther 2:6)?

_____

_____

_____

11) Read Psalm 75:6–7. What do you learn about God from these verses? How do you see these same characteristics at work in the story of Esther?

_____

_____

_____

Summing Up...

"True holiness and virtue command permanent respect and affection, far more than charm and beauty of face and form." —*John MacArthur*

Reflecting on the Text

12) What may have been the reasons that Esther and her cousin Mordecai stayed in Persia, when it seems they might have had the opportunity to return to Palestine? How was this part of God's plan for the Israelites in Persia?

_____

_____

_____

13) What's more valuable and why—wisdom (like Mordecai had) or beauty and influence (like Esther had)? When have you been jealous of another person's position, personality, or character qualities? How can you learn to be grateful for how God has made you and the ways He is using you for His glory—just the way you are?

_____

_____

_____

14) What are some of the unique experiences, positions, opportunities, and blessings that God has given you? How do you sense that He wants to use those to make an eternal difference in this world?

_____

_____

_____

_____

Recording Your Thoughts

_____

_____

_____

_____

_____

_____

For further study, see the following passages:

1 Samuel 9:1–2   2 Kings 24:14–15   2 Chronicles 36:9–10
Ezra 7:11   Daniel 1:20; 6:8, 12, 15

Haman's Plot

Opening Thought

1) A growing number of people (including many believers in Christ) are convinced of the truthfulness of all sorts of conspiracy theories involving the government, the military complex, the press, Hollywood, big banking, and even organized religion. Why do you think such theories are increasingly popular?

_____

_____

_____

_____

_____

_____

2) On a scale of 1 to 10 (with 1 meaning "totally bogus" and 10 representing "undeniably true") grade the following:

_____ that UFOs did crash in Roswell, N.M., and the military has secret proof there of extraterrestrial life

_____ that Fidel Castro or the CIA or the Mafia, or some combination, killed John F. Kennedy

_____ that the military routinely performs secret experiments on its unwitting personnel

_____ that the government has clear evidence of POWs still alive in Vietnam

_____ that most major sporting events are fixed

_____ that a small group of powerful financiers controls the world economy

Background of the Passage

Like a first-rate suspense novel, the Book of Esther, set in exotic Persia, tells the true story of rich, beautiful, and powerful people plotting and planning, striving and conniving. At stake are the lives and fortunes of both individuals and the Jewish remnant. The tension in the book is palpable. How will God get glory in such a pagan environment? How will God's people survive the hostility of their captors? Most important, what will happen to God's promises to Israel?

Through an unlikely turn of events, an attractive young Jewish woman named Esther rose to power, replacing the deposed Queen Vashti and becoming the favored wife of King Ahasuerus. Soon thereafter, Mordecai, Esther's legal guardian, learned of a plan to assassinate the king. When he revealed this plot to Esther, the would-be assassins were arrested and executed. Significantly, Mordecai's loyal act was recorded in the royal history books.

Clearly these events of chapters 1 and 2 set the stage for the crisis of chapter 3. After Mordecai rebuffed Haman, a high-ranking government official, Haman became enraged. In his thirst for revenge, he concocted a scheme to eliminate Mordecai and all the Jews. Then, without even naming the targeted people, Haman managed to get the king's approval to carry out his genocidal plot.

Continue reading and studying for a more in-depth understanding of the events of chapters 2 and 3.

Bible Passage

Read 2:21—3:15, noting the key words and definitions to the right of the passage.

Esther 2:21—3:15

21 *In those days, while Mordecai sat within the king's gate, two of the king's eunuchs, Bigthan and Teresh, doorkeepers, became furious and sought to lay hands on King Ahasuerus.*
22 *So the matter became known to Mordecai, who*

the king's gate (2:21)—indicates the strong possibility that Mordecai held a position of prominence (see 3:2)

became furious (v. 21)—perhaps in revenge over the loss of Vashti

told Queen Esther, and Esther informed the king in Mordecai's name.

23 And when an inquiry was made into the matter, it was confirmed, and both were hanged on a gallows; and it was written in the book of the chronicles in the presence of the king.

3:1 After these things King Ahasuerus promoted Haman, the son of Hammedatha the Agagite, and advanced him and set his seat above all the princes who were with him.

2 And all the king's servants who were within the king's gate bowed and paid homage to Haman, for so the king had commanded concerning him. But Mordecai would not bow or pay homage.

3 Then the king's servants who were within the king's gate said to Mordecai, "Why do you transgress the king's command?"

4 Now it happened, when they spoke to him daily and he would not listen to them, that they told it to Haman, to see whether Mordecai's words would stand; for Mordecai had told them that he was a Jew.

5 When Haman saw that Mordecai did not bow or pay him homage, Haman was filled with wrath.

6 But he disdained to lay hands on Mordecai alone, for they had told him of the people of Mordecai. Instead, Haman sought to destroy all the Jews who were throughout the whole kingdom of Ahasuerus—the people of Mordecai.

7 In the first month, which is the month of Nisan, in the twelfth year of King Ahasuerus, they cast Pur (that is, the lot), before Haman to determine the day and the month, until it fell on the twelfth month, which is the month of Adar.

8 Then Haman said to King Ahasuerus, "There is a certain people scattered and dispersed among the people in all the provinces of your kingdom; their laws are different from all other people's, and they do not keep the king's laws. Therefore it is

hanged on a gallows (v. 23)—the Persian execution consisted of being impaled; it is likely that they were the inventors of crucifixion

book of the chronicles (v. 23)—Five years later (Ahasuerus's twelfth year), the king would read these Persian records as the turning point in Esther (6:1–2).

After these things (3:1)—sometime between the seventh (2:16) and twelfth year (3:7) of the king's reign

would not bow (v. 2)—There is a question as to whether Esther and Mordecai were inclined to obey the Mosaic law. This refusal may be more likely grounded in the family feud between the Benjamites and the Agagites than in Mordecai's allegiance to the second commandment.

he was a Jew (v. 4)—It seems evident from Haman's fury and attempted genocide that there were strong anti-Semitic attitudes in Shushan, which seems to explain Mordecai's reluctance to reveal his true ethnic background.

the people of Mordecai (v. 6)—Haman was being satanically used to target the entire Jewish race in an unsuccessful attempt to change the course of redemptive history and God's plans for Israel.

Nisan (v. 7)—the time period March–April; ironically, the Jews should have been celebrating the Passover to remind them of a former deliverance

twelfth year (v. 7)—474 B.C.

they cast (v. 7)—Haman's court of advisers who made decisions superstitiously based on astrology and casting of lots

not fitting for the king to let them remain.

⁹ If it pleases the king, let a decree be written that they be destroyed, and I will pay ten thousand talents of silver into the hands of those who do the work, to bring it into the king's treasuries."

¹⁰ So the king took his signet ring from his hand and gave it to Haman, the son of Hammedatha the Agagite, the enemy of the Jews.

¹¹ And the king said to Haman, "The money and the people are given to you, to do with them as seems good to you."

¹² Then the king's scribes were called on the thirteenth day of the first month, and a decree was written according to all that Haman commanded—to the king's satraps, to the governors who were over each province, to the officials of all people, to every province according to its script, and to every people in their language. In the name of King Ahasuerus it was written, and sealed with the king's signet ring.

¹³ And the letters were sent by couriers into all the king's provinces, to destroy, to kill, and to annihilate all the Jews, both young and old, little children and women, in one day, on the thirteenth day of the twelfth month, which is the month of Adar, and to plunder their possessions.

¹⁴ A copy of the document was to be issued as law in every province, being published for all people, that they should be ready for that day.

¹⁵ The couriers went out, hastened by the king's command; and the decree was proclaimed in Shushan the citadel. So the king and Haman sat down to drink, but the city of Shushan was perplexed.

Pur . . . lot (v. 7)—A "lot" would be like modern dice; they were cast to determine future decisions (see Jonah 1:7).

Adar (v. 7)—February–March; eleven months would have passed between Haman's decree and its expected fulfillment

a certain people (v. 8)—Haman never divulged their identity.

ten thousand talents (v. 9)—The exact amount in dollars is uncertain, but reportedly it would have weighed 375 tons and equaled almost 70 percent of the king's annual revenue. Since this sum would have been derived from the plunder of the Jews, it indicates that they had grown prosperous.

the enemy of the Jews (v. 10)—see 7:6; 8:1; 9:10, 24

sealed . . . king's signet ring (v. 12)—This would be equivalent to the king's signature. The date has been calculated by historians to be April 7, 474 B.C.

to destroy (v. 13)—an ambitious plot to annihilate the Jews in just one day; historians have calculated the date to be March 7, 473 B.C.; the king had unwittingly approved this provision that would kill his own queen

as law (v. 14)—It would be irrevocable (see 1:19; 8:5–8).

perplexed (v. 15)—No specific reason is stated. Most likely even this pagan population was puzzled at the extreme and deadly racism of the king and Haman.

Understanding the Text

3) What were the details of the plot to assassinate King Ahasuerus? How did Mordecai thwart this plot?

_____

_____

_____

_____

_____

4) Why did Haman become furious with Mordecai? Why do you think Mordecai refused to pay homage to Haman?

_____

_____

_____

_____

_____

(verses to consider: Exodus 20:3–6; Deuteronomy 25:17–19; 1 Samuel 15:32–33; Matthew 4:10)

5) How did Haman try to determine a date on which to carry out his murderous plot? How do you see God's sovereign hand at work through this process? Why don't we use this method for making decisions today? What resources has God given us to help us make decisions?

_____

_____

_____

_____

_____

(verses to consider: Nehemiah 10:34; Proverbs 16:33; Acts 1:26)

Cross-Reference

Read Daniel 6.

1 *It pleased Darius to set over the kingdom one hundred and twenty satraps, to be over the whole kingdom;*

2 *and over these, three governors, of whom Daniel was one, that the satraps might give account to them, so that the king would suffer no loss.*

3 *Then this Daniel distinguished himself above the governors and satraps, because an excellent spirit was in him; and the king gave thought to setting him over the whole realm.*

4 *So the governors and satraps sought to find some charge against Daniel concerning the kingdom; but they could find no charge or fault, because he was faithful; nor was there any error or fault found in him.*

5 *Then these men said, "We shall not find any charge against this Daniel unless we find it against him concerning the law of his God."*

6 *So these governors and satraps thronged before the king, and said thus to him: "King Darius, live forever!*

7 *All the governors of the kingdom, the administrators and satraps, the counselors and advisors, have consulted together to establish a royal statute and to make a firm decree, that whoever petitions any god or man for thirty days, except you, O king, shall be cast into the den of lions.*

8 *Now, O king, establish the decree and sign the writing, so that it cannot be changed, according to the law of the Medes and Persians, which does not alter."*

9 *Therefore King Darius signed the written decree.*

10 *Now when Daniel knew that the writing was signed, he went home. And in his upper room, with his windows open toward Jerusalem, he knelt down on his knees three times that day, and prayed and gave thanks before his God, as was his custom since early days.*

11 *Then these men assembled and found Daniel praying and making supplication before his God.*

12 *And they went before the king, and spoke concerning the king's decree: "Have you not signed a decree that every man who petitions any god or man within thirty days, except you, O king, shall be cast into the den of lions?" The king answered and said, "The thing is true, according to the law of the Medes and Persians, which does not alter."*

13 *So they answered and said before the king, "That Daniel, who is one of the captives from Judah, does not show due regard for you, O king, or for the decree that you have signed, but makes his petition three times a day."*

¹⁴ *And the king, when he heard these words, was greatly displeased with himself, and set his heart on Daniel to deliver him; and he labored till the going down of the sun to deliver him.*

¹⁵ *Then these men approached the king, and said to the king, "Know, O king, that it is the law of the Medes and Persians that no decree or statute which the king establishes may be changed."*

¹⁶ *So the king gave the command, and they brought Daniel and cast him into the den of lions. But the king spoke, saying to Daniel, "Your God, whom you serve continually, He will deliver you."*

¹⁷ *Then a stone was brought and laid on the mouth of the den, and the king sealed it with his own signet ring and with the signets of his lords, that the purpose concerning Daniel might not be changed.*

¹⁸ *Now the king went to his palace and spent the night fasting; and no musicians were brought before him. Also his sleep went from him.*

¹⁹ *Then the king arose very early in the morning and went in haste to the den of lions.*

²⁰ *And when he came to the den, he cried out with a lamenting voice to Daniel. The king spoke, saying to Daniel, "Daniel, servant of the living God, has your God, whom you serve continually, been able to deliver you from the lions?"*

²¹ *Then Daniel said to the king, "O king, live forever!*

²² *My God sent His angel and shut the lions' mouths, so that they have not hurt me, because I was found innocent before Him; and also, O king, I have done no wrong before you."*

²³ *Then the king was exceedingly glad for him, and commanded that they should take Daniel up out of the den. So Daniel was taken up out of the den, and no injury whatever was found on him, because he believed in his God.*

²⁴ *And the king gave the command, and they brought those men who had accused Daniel, and they cast them into the den of lions—them, their children, and their wives; and the lions overpowered them, and broke all their bones in pieces before they ever came to the bottom of the den.*

²⁵ *Then King Darius wrote: To all peoples, nations, and languages that dwell in all the earth: Peace be multiplied to you.*

²⁶ *I make a decree that in every dominion of my kingdom men must tremble and fear before the God of Daniel. For He is the living God, and steadfast forever; His kingdom is the one which shall not be destroyed, and His dominion shall endure to the end.*

²⁷ *He delivers and rescues, and He works signs and wonders in heaven and on earth, Who has delivered Daniel from the power of the lions.*

²⁸ *So this Daniel prospered in the reign of Darius and in the reign of Cyrus the Persian.*

6) In what ways do the stories of Esther 3 and Daniel 6 parallel each other?

_____

_____

_____

Exploring the Meaning

7) Read Acts 4:13–22 and 5:17–29. Why is it common for those in positions of power to try to muzzle or control the people of God?

_____

_____

_____

_____

_____

8) Read Jehoshaphat's prayer in 2 Chronicles 20:5–12. In what ways is this a model prayer for any child of God who is in trouble?

_____

_____

_____

_____

_____

Summing Up...

"Because our God is infinite in power and love, we confidently say, 'The Lord is my helper, I will not fear. What can man do to me?' (Hebrews 13:6). Because our God is infinite in power and love, we can say with David, 'Whenever I am afraid, I will trust in You' (Psalm 56:3) and, 'I will both lie down in peace and sleep; for You alone, O Lord, make me dwell in safety' (Psalm 4:8). Because our God is infinite in power and love, we can say with Moses, 'The eternal God is your refuge, and underneath are the everlasting arms' (Deuteronomy 33:27). Because our God is infinite in power and love, we can say with the writer of Hebrews, 'This hope we have as an anchor of the soul, both sure and steadfast' (Hebrews 6:19)."—*John MacArthur*

Reflecting on the Text

9) In what specific ways have you been pressured to compromise your faith?

_____

_____

_____

_____

_____

10) What do you think precipitated such an extreme response on the part of Haman?

_____

_____

_____

_____

_____

11) The population of Shushan (or Susa) was "perplexed" by the decision of the king (3:15). What would you say are the most perplexing issues with which our citizens struggle? Why?

_____

_____

_____

_____

_____

Recording Your Thoughts

_____

_____

_____

_____

_____

_____

_____

_____

_____

_____

_____

_____

For further study, see the following passages:

Exodus 20:4–6   Ezra 6:11   Daniel 2:49

Mordecai's Plan

Opening Thought

1) In a crisis situation, how do you typically respond? Do you (a) become hysterical; (b) become immobilized by fear; (c) pray; (d) swing into action; (e) try to escape; (f) react in some other way? Why do you think you respond this way?

_____

_____

_____

2) What are some of the most courageous decisions you witnessed in the last year? What tough, but right, choices have you made yourself? What happened?

_____

_____

_____

_____

3) Do you think it is difficult for Western Christians to really iden-tify with stories in which people of faith face death because of their beliefs? Why?

_____

_____

_____

_____

Background of the Passage

Following the seventy-year exile period, the Jews were given permission to return to their homeland. Some had done so under the leadership of Zerubbabel and had begun to rebuild the temple (see Ezra). Another large group had remained in Persia. Among them were a beautiful young woman named Esther and her cousin/adopted father, Mordecai.

When Vashti, the queen of Persia, defied an order of King Ahasuerus, she was deposed and a search was begun for a new queen. Somehow, Esther, keeping her Jewish heritage a secret, was included in this royal contest; eventually she became the surprise winner. Meanwhile, Mordecai uncovered a plot to assassinate the king. Through Esther he was able to get word to the palace and the would-be evildoers were brought to justice.

The plot thickened when a high-ranking official named Haman, angered by Mordecai's refusal to bow to him, concocted a scheme to eradicate all the Jews in Persia. When the king agreed to Haman's murderous plan, the only question remaining was whether Esther could use her position of influence to save her people. That is the situation in chapter 4.

Read the passage carefully and imagine yourself in Esther's or Mordecai's situation. Let the drama of their crisis wash over you. Try to appreciate the great pressure they felt. And let God use this real-life situation from centuries past to change you today.

Bible Passage

Read 4:1–17, noting the key words and definitions to the right of the passage.

Esther 4:1–17

1 *When Mordecai learned all that had happened, he tore his clothes and put on sackcloth and ashes, and went out into the midst of the city. He cried out with a loud and bitter cry.*

2 *He went as far as the front of the king's gate, for no one might enter the king's gate clothed with sackcloth.*

sackcloth and ashes (v. 1)— an outward sign of inward distress and humiliation; Mordecai realized that he had prompted this genocidal retaliation by Haman

³ And in every province where the king's command and decree arrived, there was great mourning among the Jews, with fasting, weeping, and wailing; and many lay in sackcloth and ashes.

⁴ So Esther's maids and eunuchs came and told her, and the queen was deeply distressed. Then she sent garments to clothe Mordecai and take his sackcloth away from him, but he would not accept them.

⁵ Then Esther called Hathach, one of the king's eunuchs whom he had appointed to attend her, and she gave him a command concerning Mordecai, to learn what and why this was.

⁶ So Hathach went out to Mordecai in the city square that was in front of the king's gate.

⁷ And Mordecai told him all that had happened to him, and the sum of money that Haman had promised to pay into the king's treasuries to destroy the Jews.

⁸ He also gave him a copy of the written decree for their destruction, which was given at Shushan, that he might show it to Esther and explain it to her, and that he might command her to go in to the king to make supplication to him and plead before him for her people.

⁹ So Hathach returned and told Esther the words of Mordecai.

¹⁰ Then Esther spoke to Hathach, and gave him a command for Mordecai:

¹¹ "All the king's servants and the people of the king's provinces know that any man or woman who goes into the inner court to the king, who has not been called, he has but one law: put all to death, except the one to whom the king holds out the golden scepter, that he may live. Yet I myself have not been called to go in to the king these thirty days."

¹² So they told Mordecai Esther's words.

¹³ And Mordecai told them to answer Esther: "Do

she sent garments (v. 4)—Mordecai could then enter the king's gate (see 4:2) and talk with Esther directly.

Hathach (v. 5)—a trusted eunuch who knew of Esther's Jewish background

He also gave him a copy of the written decree (v. 8)—That Mordecai possessed this specific knowledge and a copy of the edict further evidences his prominent position in Persia.

golden scepter (v. 11)—In order to protect the king's life from would-be assassins, this practice prevailed; seemingly, the king would extend the scepter (a sign of kingly authority) only to those whom he knew and from whom he welcomed a visit (see 5:2; 8:4).

these thirty days (v. 11)—Perhaps Esther feared she had lost favor with the king since he had not summoned her recently.

not think in your heart that you will escape in the king's palace any more than all the other Jews.

14 For if you remain completely silent at this time, relief and deliverance will arise for the Jews from another place, but you and your father's house will perish. Yet who knows whether you have come to the kingdom for such a time as this?"

15 Then Esther told them to reply to Mordecai:

16 "Go, gather all the Jews who are present in Shushan, and fast for me; neither eat nor drink for three days, night or day. My maids and I will fast likewise. And so I will go to the king, which is against the law; and if I perish, I perish!"

17 So Mordecai went his way and did according to all that Esther commanded him.

relief and deliverance (v. 14) —Mordecai exhibited a healthy faith in God's sovereign power to preserve His people. He may have remembered the Lord's promise to Abraham (see Genesis 12:3; 17:1–8).

you . . . will perish (v. 14)— Mordecai indicated that Esther because of her prominence, would not escape the sentence or be overlooked (see 4:13).

such a time as this (v. 14)— Mordecai indirectly appealed to God's providential timing.

fast (v. 16)—The text does not mention prayer being included, though surely it was.

perish (v. 16)—Esther's heroic willingness to die for the sake of her fellow Jews is commendable.

Understanding the Text

4) How did Mordecai respond when he learned that Haman's genocidal decree had been approved by the king? What is the significance of sackcloth and ashes? Can you think of any modern-day equivalents for believers in the West?

_____

_____

_____

_____

(verses to consider: Genesis 37:34; 2 Kings 19:1; Jeremiah 6:26; Daniel 9:3)

5) The chapter makes a couple of references to fasting (verses 3, 16). What is the purpose of fasting? What does it indicate?

_____

_____

_____

_____

_____

(verses to consider: Ezra 8:21; 9:5; Nehemiah 1:4; Psalm 35:13)

6) What did Mordecai want Esther to do? Why was she fearful of his request? What finally convinced her to approach the king?

_____

_____

_____

_____

7) What is significant about Mordecai's claim that if you remain completely silent at this time, relief and deliverance will arise for the Jews from another place (verse 14)?

_____

_____

_____

_____

(verses to consider: Genesis 17:1–8)

Cross-Reference

Read Daniel 3.

[1] *Nebuchadnezzar the king made an image of gold, whose height was sixty cubits and its width six cubits. He set it up in the plain of Dura, in the province of Babylon.*

² *And King Nebuchadnezzar sent word to gather together the satraps, the administrators, the governors, the counselors, the treasurers, the judges, the magistrates, and all the officials of the provinces, to come to the dedication of the image which King Nebuchadnezzar had set up.*

³ *So the satraps, the administrators, the governors, the counselors, the treasurers, the judges, the magistrates, and all the officials of the provinces gathered together for the dedication of the image that King Nebuchadnezzar had set up; and they stood before the image that Nebuchadnezzar had set up.*

⁴ *Then a herald cried aloud: "To you it is commanded, O peoples, nations, and languages,*

⁵ *that at the time you hear the sound of the horn, flute, harp, lyre, and psaltery, in symphony with all kinds of music, you shall fall down and worship the gold image that King Nebuchadnezzar has set up;*

⁶ *and whoever does not fall down and worship shall be cast immediately into the midst of a burning fiery furnace."*

⁷ *So at that time, when all the people heard the sound of the horn, flute, harp, and lyre, in symphony with all kinds of music, all the people, nations, and languages fell down and worshiped the gold image which King Nebuchadnezzar had set up.*

⁸ *Therefore at that time certain Chaldeans came forward and accused the Jews.*

⁹ *They spoke and said to King Nebuchadnezzar, "O king, live forever!*

¹⁰ *You, O king, have made a decree that everyone who hears the sound of the horn, flute, harp, lyre, and psaltery, in symphony with all kinds of music, shall fall down and worship the gold image;*

¹¹ *and whoever does not fall down and worship shall be cast into the midst of a burning fiery furnace.*

¹² *There are certain Jews whom you have set over the affairs of the province of Babylon: Shadrach, Meshach, and Abed-Nego; these men, O king, have not paid due regard to you. They do not serve your gods or worship the gold image which you have set up."*

¹³ *Then Nebuchadnezzar, in rage and fury, gave the command to bring Shadrach, Meshach, and Abed-Nego. So they brought these men before the king.*

¹⁴ *Nebuchadnezzar spoke, saying to them, "Is it true, Shadrach, Meshach, and Abed-Nego, that you do not serve my gods or worship the gold image which I have set up?*

¹⁵ *Now if you are ready at the time you hear the sound of the horn, flute, harp, lyre, and psaltery, in symphony with all kinds of music, and you fall down and worship the image which I have made, good! But if you do not worship, you shall be cast immediately into the midst of a burning fiery furnace. And who is the god who will deliver you from my hands?"*

¹⁶ *Shadrach, Meshach, and Abed-Nego answered and said to the king, "O*

Nebuchadnezzar, we have no need to answer you in this matter.

17 *If that is the case, our God whom we serve is able to deliver us from the burning fiery furnace, and He will deliver us from your hand, O king.*

18 *But if not, let it be known to you, O king, that we do not serve your gods, nor will we worship the gold image which you have set up."*

19 *Then Nebuchadnezzar was full of fury, and the expression on his face changed toward Shadrach, Meshach, and Abed-Nego. He spoke and commanded that they heat the furnace seven times more than it was usually heated.*

20 *And he commanded certain mighty men of valor who were in his army to bind Shadrach, Meshach, and Abed-Nego, and cast them into the burning fiery furnace.*

21 *Then these men were bound in their coats, their trousers, their turbans, and their other garments, and were cast into the midst of the burning fiery furnace.*

22 *Therefore, because the king's command was urgent, and the furnace exceedingly hot, the flame of the fire killed those men who took up Shadrach, Meshach, and Abed-Nego.*

23 *And these three men, Shadrach, Meshach, and Abed-Nego, fell down bound into the midst of the burning fiery furnace.*

24 *Then King Nebuchadnezzar was astonished; and he rose in haste and spoke, saying to his counselors, "Did we not cast three men bound into the midst of the fire?" They answered and said to the king, "True, O king."*

25 *"Look!" he answered, "I see four men loose, walking in the midst of the fire; and they are not hurt, and the form of the fourth is like the Son of God."*

26 *Then Nebuchadnezzar went near the mouth of the burning fiery furnace and spoke, saying, "Shadrach, Meshach, and Abed-Nego, servants of the Most High God, come out, and come here." Then Shadrach, Meshach, and Abed-Nego came from the midst of the fire.*

27 *And the satraps, administrators, governors, and the king's counselors gathered together, and they saw these men on whose bodies the fire had no power; the hair of their head was not singed nor were their garments affected, and the smell of fire was not on them.*

28 *Nebuchadnezzar spoke, saying, "Blessed be the God of Shadrach, Meshach, and Abed-Nego, who sent His Angel and delivered His servants who trusted in Him, and they have frustrated the king's word, and yielded their bodies, that they should not serve nor worship any god except their own God!*

29 *Therefore I make a decree that any people, nation, or language which speaks anything amiss against the God of Shadrach, Meshach, and Abed-Nego shall be cut in pieces, and their houses shall be made an ash heap; because there is no other God who can deliver like this."*

30 *Then the king promoted Shadrach, Meshach, and Abed-Nego in the province of Babylon.*

8) How is Esther's classic statement of courage, "If I perish, I perish," similar to the response of Shadrach, Meshach, and Abed-Nego to King Nebuchadnezzar?

_____

_____

_____

_____

Exploring the Meaning

9) Read Acts 20:22–24. Did the threat of punishment or suffering deter Paul? Why or why not?

_____

_____

_____

_____

_____

10) Read Philippians 2:3–4. In what ways did Esther "live out" the truth of this New Testament passage? How might her privileged life in the luxury of the Persian royal palace have altered her values and affected her actions?

_____

_____

_____

_____

_____

_____

Summing Up...

"When the things of this world are idolized, as they frequently are even by believers, it is impossible not to be drawn into the moral and spiritual compromises that such idolatry demands. When a person longs to be like the world... he soon will be thinking and acting like it."
—John MacArthur

Reflecting on the Text

11) Mordecai essentially reasoned with Esther this way: "Do you think your becoming queen of Persia was a mere fluke? Do you think you can now ignore your heritage and opt only to live a comfortable life? No, there's a reason you've been placed in such an influential position! You need to take careful stock of this situation and use it to the glory of God."

If you had a wise old "Cousin Mordecai," what counsel might he give you today as you face your unique life situation?

_____

_____

_____

_____

_____

12) Think of someone, perhaps a younger Christian, who needs some Mordecai-like encouragement and exhortation. What can you say or do to stir up that person to "love and good works" (Hebrews 10:24)?

_____

_____

_____

_____

_____

Recording Your Thoughts

_____

_____

_____

_____

_____

_____

_____

_____

_____

_____

_____

_____

_____

_____

_____

_____

_____

_____

_____

_____

For further study, see the following passages:

Genesis 12:1	Nehemiah 2:2	Psalm 109:24
Isaiah 37:1	Daniel 9:3	Joel 2:12
Jonah 3:5	Matthew 11:21	

Esther's Intercession

Opening Thought

1) If you could ask any person for any favor (and you knew it would be granted), whom would you approach and what would you request? Why?

_____

_____

_____

_____

2) What does the word "intercession" mean?

_____

_____

_____

3) What giant requests to God do you consistently make on behalf of others?

_____

_____

_____

_____

_____

_____

Background of the Passage

Ezra, Nehemiah, and Esther give an account of what happened to the Jewish people following their seventy-year exile. Ezra is essentially a book about restoration. Chapters 1–6 describe Zerubbabel's attempt to rebuild the temple (538–515 B.C.), and chapters 7–10 speak of a spiritual revival sparked by Ezra (457 B.C.). Nehemiah is a book about reconstruction, describing the rebuilding of the walls of Jerusalem (444–425 B.C.). Esther, meanwhile, is a book about preservation, telling what happened to the Jews who remained behind in Persia (sometime between the years of 515–457 B.C.).

The story of chapters 1–4 of Esther is this: Through a series of God-ordained events, the queen of Persia was deposed after defying the king. After a beauty contest of sorts was held in order to find a new queen, a young Jewish girl named Esther was the surprise winner.

When Esther's cousin Mordecai offended a high-ranking government official, that official, Haman, vengefully enacted a plan to exterminate the Jews. Humanly speaking, only Esther was in a position to influence the king to rescind his decree. She must somehow intercede for her people. And given the king's willingness to impulsively replace any queen who displeases him, Esther faced very real risks.

Following the counsel of her uncle, Esther bravely agreed to do what she could. Esther 4:16 says: "Go, gather all the Jews who are present in Shushan, and fast for me; neither eat nor drink for three days, night or day. My maids and I will fast likewise. And so I will go to the king, which is against the law; and if I perish, I perish!"

Bible Passage

Read 5:1–8, noting the key words and definitions to the right of the passage.

Esther 5:1–8

1 *Now it happened on the third day that Esther put on her royal robes and stood in the inner court of the king's palace, across from the king's house, while the king sat on his royal throne in the royal house, facing the entrance of the house.*

² So it was, when the king saw Queen Esther standing in the court, that she found favor in his sight, and the king held out to Esther the golden scepter that was in his hand. Then Esther went near and touched the top of the scepter.

³ And the king said to her, "What do you wish, Queen Esther? What is your request? It shall be given to you—up to half the kingdom!"

⁴ So Esther answered, "If it pleases the king, let the king and Haman come today to the banquet that I have prepared for him."

⁵ Then the king said, "Bring Haman quickly, that he may do as Esther has said." So the king and Haman went to the banquet that Esther had prepared.

⁶ At the banquet of wine the king said to Esther, "What is your petition? It shall be granted you. What is your request, up to half the kingdom? It shall be done!"

⁷ Then Esther answered and said, "My petition and request is this:

⁸ If I have found favor in the sight of the king, and if it pleases the king to grant my petition and fulfill my request, then let the king and Haman come to the banquet which I will prepare for them, and tomorrow I will do as the king has said."

she found favor (v. 2)—This actually means that Esther first found favor with the God of Israel.

What is your request? (v. 3) —Esther deferred her real wish until 7:2–3.

sup to half the kingdom (vv. 3–6)—royal hyperbole that was not intended to be taken at face value

the banquet (v. 4)—the first of two (see 5:4–8; 6:14—7:1) that Esther prepared; God would providentially intervene between the two (6:1–2)

Understanding the Text

4) What was risky about Esther's plan and actions?

_____

_____

_____

_____

5) Esther was obviously favored by the king—he had hand-picked her from among the most desirable women in Persia. What do you think made her afraid (or at least timid) to intercede for her people?

_____

_____

_____

6) Why do you think Esther invited the king and Haman to elaborate back-to-back banquets, rather than just coming right out with her petition? Why the second banquet?

_____

_____

_____

Cross-Reference

Read Romans 8:26–39.

26 *Likewise the Spirit also helps in our weaknesses. For we do not know what we should pray for as we ought, but the Spirit Himself makes intercession for us with groanings which cannot be uttered.*

27 *Now He who searches the hearts knows what the mind of the Spirit is, because He makes intercession for the saints according to the will of God.*

28 *And we know that all things work together for good to those who love God, to those who are the called according to His purpose.*

29 *For whom He foreknew, He also predestined to be conformed to the image of His Son, that He might be the firstborn among many brethren.*

30 *Moreover whom He predestined, these He also called; whom He called, these He also justified; and whom He justified, these He also glorified.*

31 *What then shall we say to these things? If God is for us, who can be against us?*

32 *He who did not spare His own Son, but delivered Him up for us all, how shall He not with Him also freely give us all things?*

33 *Who shall bring a charge against God's elect? It is God who justifies.*

34 *Who is he who condemns? It is Christ who died, and furthermore is also risen, who is even at the right hand of God, who also makes intercession for us.*

³⁵ *Who shall separate us from the love of Christ? Shall tribulation, or distress, or persecution, or famine, or nakedness, or peril, or sword?*

³⁶ *As it is written: "For Your sake we are killed all day long; we are accounted as sheep for the slaughter."*

³⁷ *Yet in all these things we are more than conquerors through Him who loved us.*

³⁸ *For I am persuaded that neither death nor life, nor angels nor principalities nor powers, nor things present nor things to come,*

³⁹ *nor height nor depth, nor any other created thing, shall be able to separate us from the love of God which is in Christ Jesus our Lord.*

7) What does this passage teach about intercession? Who is doing the interceding in this passage?

_____

_____

_____

Exploring the Meaning

8) Read Exodus 32:7–14. Why did Moses intercede for the people of Israel in this passage? What happened as a result?

_____

_____

_____

9) Read Ephesians 6:18–19. How and why should we intercede for other believers?

_____

_____

_____

_____

(verses to consider: 1 Samuel 12:23; Colossians 4:12; 1 Timothy 2:1)

Summing Up...

"Most Christians never get serious about prayer until a problem arises in their own life or in the life of someone they love. Then they are inclined to pray intently, specifically, and persistently. Yet that is the way Christians should always pray. Sensitivity to the problems and needs of others, especially other believers who are facing trials or hardships, will lead us to pray for them 'night and day' as Paul did for Timothy (2 Timothy 1:3)."—*John MacArthur*

Reflecting on the Text

10) Can you think of a recent situation in which you needed courage to do something difficult or risky? What happened?

_____

_____

_____

11) Who in your sphere of influence needs your intercessory prayer today? How can you use your position with the King of kings (Hebrews 4:16) to make a difference in another's life?

_____

_____

_____

Recording Your Thoughts

_____

_____

_____

For further study, see the following passages:

Proverbs 21:1	Mark 6:22–23	Romans 1:9; 15:30
Philippians 1:3–4	Hebrews 7:25	1 Peter 3:12

Haman's Humiliation

Opening Thought

1) How would you define "pride"? What is "humble pie"?

_____

_____

_____

_____

_____

_____

2) Is there a such a thing as "good pride"? Why or why not?

_____

_____

_____

_____

_____

_____

_____

_____

Background of the Passage

In his masterwork *Mere Christianity*, C. S. Lewis called pride "the great sin" and wrote: "The essential vice, the utmost evil, is Pride. Unchastity, anger, greed, drunkenness, and all that, are mere fleabites in comparison: it was through Pride that the devil became the devil: Pride leads to every other vice: it is the complete anti-God state of mind. . . . As long as you are proud you cannot know God at all. A proud man is always looking down on things and people: and, of course, as long as you are looking down, you cannot see something that is above you." (New York, NY: Collier Books/MacMillan Publishing Co., 1943, 1945, 1952, pp. 94, 96).

The Book of Esther offers a classic case study of the sin and consequences of pride. Haman was an Agagite, a prominent government official in Persia. Because he had been snubbed by an exiled Jew named Mordecai, Haman used his power and influence to secure a royal decree calling for the extermination of all Jews.

What the arrogant Haman didn't know was that years earlier, Mordecai had saved the king's life and that Mordecai's young cousin was Queen Esther! Together these two facts would cause Haman's murderous plot to quickly unravel. In fact, the tables would be utterly turned, proving that "pride goes before destruction, and a haughty spirit before a fall" (Proverbs 16:18).

Bible Passage

Read 5:9—6:14, noting the key words and definitions to the right of the passage.

Esther 5:9—6:14

9 *So Haman went out that day joyful and with a glad heart; but when Haman saw Mordecai in the king's gate, and that he did not stand or tremble before him, he was filled with indignation against Mordecai.*

10 *Nevertheless Haman restrained himself and went*

home, and he sent and called for his friends and his wife Zeresh.

11 Then Haman told them of his great riches, the multitude of his children, everything in which the king had promoted him, and how he had advanced him above the officials and servants of the king.

12 Moreover Haman said, "Besides, Queen Esther invited no one but me to come in with the king to the banquet that she prepared; and tomorrow I am again invited by her, along with the king.

13 Yet all this avails me nothing, so long as I see Mordecai the Jew sitting at the king's gate."

14 Then his wife Zeresh and all his friends said to him, "Let a gallows be made, fifty cubits high, and in the morning suggest to the king that Mordecai be hanged on it; then go merrily with the king to the banquet." And the thing pleased Haman; so he had the gallows made.

6:1 That night the king could not sleep. So one was commanded to bring the book of the records of the chronicles; and they were read before the king.

2 And it was found written that Mordecai had told of Bigthana and Teresh, two of the king's eunuchs, the doorkeepers who had sought to lay hands on King Ahasuerus.

3 Then the king said, "What honor or dignity has been bestowed on Mordecai for this?" And the king's servants who attended him said, "Nothing has been done for him."

4 So the king said, "Who is in the court?" Now Haman had just entered the outer court of the king's palace to suggest that the king hang Mordecai on the gallows that he had prepared for him.

5 The king's servants said to him, "Haman is there, standing in the court." And the king said, "Let him come in."

6 So Haman came in, and the king asked him,

the multitude of his children (v. 11)—At least ten sons were fathered by Haman (see 9:13), who personified sinful pride (see Galatians 6:3).

avails me nothing (v. 13)—Haman expressed raging fixation on killing Mordecai.

gallows (v. 14)—a stake on which a human would be impaled to death or displayed after death (see 2:23).

fifty cubits (v. 14)—approximately 75 feet or almost eight stories high; perhaps the gallows involved displaying a shorter stake atop a building or wall to attain this height.

the book (6:1)—Five years (see 2:16 with 3:7) had past since Mordecai's loyal, but as yet unrewarded, act (see 2:23). At exactly the proper moment, God providentially intervened so that the king suffered insomnia, called for the book of records, read of Mordecai's unrewarded deeds five years earlier, and then desired to reward him (see Daniel 6:18).

Who is in the court? (v. 4)—The drama intensified as Haman arrived at just the wrong time and for just the wrong reason.

Whom would the king delight to honor more than me? (v. 6)—Haman ironically defined the honor to be given to Mordecai at Haman's expense. To his potential wealth from the Jewish plunder, he thought public acclaim would be added.

"What shall be done for the man whom the king delights to honor?" Now Haman thought in his heart, "Whom would the king delight to honor more than me?"

7 And Haman answered the king, "For the man whom the king delights to honor,

8 Let a royal robe be brought which the king has worn, and a horse on which the king has ridden, which has a royal crest placed on its head.

9 Then let this robe and horse be delivered to the hand of one of the king's most noble princes, that he may array the man whom the king delights to honor. Then parade him on horseback through the city square, and proclaim before him: 'Thus shall it be done to the man whom the king delights to honor!'"

10 Then the king said to Haman, "Hurry, take the robe and the horse, as you have suggested, and do so for Mordecai the Jew who sits within the king's gate! Leave nothing undone of all that you have spoken."

11 So Haman took the robe and the horse, arrayed Mordecai and led him on horseback through the city square, and proclaimed before him, "Thus shall it be done to the man whom the king delights to honor!"

12 Afterward Mordecai went back to the king's gate. But Haman hurried to his house, mourning and with his head covered.

13 When Haman told his wife Zeresh and all his friends everything that had happened to him, his wise men and his wife Zeresh said to him, "If Mordecai, before whom you have begun to fall, is of Jewish descent, you will not prevail against him but will surely fall before him."

14 While they were still talking with him, the king's eunuchs came, and hastened to bring Haman to the banquet which Esther had prepared.

royal robe . . . royal crest (v. 8)—an honor which involved being treated as though the recipient were the king himself (see 8:15); this is reminiscent of Joseph in Egypt; history affirms that horses were adorned with the royal crown

the city square (v. 9)—Mordecai had been there the day before in sackcloth and ashes (Esther 4:6); this time he arrived with royal honor.

Mordecai the Jew (v. 10)—See 8:7; 9:29, 31; 10:3. Why the king did not remember Haman's edict against the Jews remains unknown.

mourning (v. 12)—Deservedly, Haman inherited Mordecai's distress (see 4:1–2). What a difference a day makes! His imagined honors had quickly turned to unimaginable humiliation.

his head covered (v. 12)—an extreme sign of shame (see 2 Samuel 15:30)

you have begun to fall (v. 13)—Neither divine prophecy (Exodus 17:14) nor biblical history (1 Samuel 15:8, 9) stood in Haman's favor. Haman's entourage seemed to have some knowledge of this biblical history.

Haman to the banquet (v. 14)—Like a lamb led to slaughter, Haman was escorted off to his just due.

Understanding the Text

3) What made Haman so proud? So angry?

_____

_____

_____

_____

(verses to consider: Proverbs 11:2; Habakkuk 2:4; 2 Timothy 3:2)

4) What were Haman's expectations? What counsel did he receive from family and friends?

_____

_____

_____

5) To what do you attribute the king's sleeplessness? Why?

_____

_____

_____

6) What happened when Haman realized the king intended to honor Mordecai instead? What words do you think accurately describe Haman's internal state?

_____

_____

_____

_____

Cross-Reference

Read Daniel 4:28–37.

28 *All this came upon King Nebuchadnezzar.*

29 *At the end of the twelve months he was walking about the royal palace of Babylon.*

30 *The king spoke, saying, "Is not this great Babylon, that I have built for a royal dwelling by my mighty power and for the honor of my majesty?"*

31 *While the word was still in the king's mouth, a voice fell from heaven: "King Nebuchadnezzar, to you it is spoken: the kingdom has departed from you!*

32 *And they shall drive you from men, and your dwelling shall be with the beasts of the field. They shall make you eat grass like oxen; and seven times shall pass over you, until you know that the Most High rules in the kingdom of men, and gives it to whomever He chooses."*

33 *That very hour the word was fulfilled concerning Nebuchadnezzar; he was driven from men and ate grass like oxen; his body was wet with the dew of heaven till his hair had grown like eagles' feathers and his nails like birds' claws.*

34 *And at the end of the time I, Nebuchadnezzar, lifted my eyes to heaven, and my understanding returned to me; and I blessed the Most High and praised and honored Him who lives forever: For His dominion is an everlasting dominion, And His kingdom is from generation to generation.*

35 *All the inhabitants of the earth are reputed as nothing; He does according to His will in the army of heaven And among the inhabitants of the earth. No one can restrain His hand Or say to Him, "What have You done?"*

36 *At the same time my reason returned to me, and for the glory of my kingdom, my honor and splendor returned to me. My counselors and nobles resorted to me, I was restored to my kingdom, and excellent majesty was added to me.*

37 *Now I, Nebuchadnezzar, praise and extol and honor the King of heaven, all of whose works are truth, and His ways justice. And those who walk in pride He is able to put down.*

7) In what ways were Haman's and Nebuchadnezzar's experiences alike? How were they different?

_____

_____

_____

Exploring the Meaning

8) Read Proverbs 16:18. If Haman had read this verse and applied it to his life, how would his actions have been different?

_____

_____

_____

_____

9) Read James 4:6–10. What does this passage say to those who are proud in heart? What does it promise to the humble?

_____

_____

_____

_____

Summing Up...

"Pride is a universal and deadly sin. It is the most characteristic and controlling sin in all human fallenness. Pride is an easy sin to indulge in, since it does not entail the loss of public reputation, prestige, health, or wealth associated with other socially unacceptable sins. Pride, in fact, has been redefined as a virtue. Sinful pride often masquerades under seemingly upright motives. In Herod, it masked itself as integrity and beheaded John the Baptist. In the Pharisees, it masked itself as holiness and rejected the Holy One. Among the Jewish authorities, it masked itself as zeal for God and executed the Son of God.

"Pride cost man Eden, and the fallen angels heaven. It doomed Sodom and Gormorrah. It cost Nebuchadnezzar his reason, Rehoboam his kingdom, Uzziah his health, and Haman his life."—*John MacArthur*

Reflecting on the Text

10) Clearly God was in control of this harrowing situation from start to finish. He caused the sleeplessness of the king, He orchestrated the events which led to the king's discovery of Mordecai's earlier loyalty. Describe some similar "coincidences" in your past which prove God's sovereignty over your life.

_____

_____

_____

11) In what areas of your life are you most tempted to become cocky or arrogant? Why? Put another way, if God desired to humble you, where do you think He might focus His attention?

_____

_____

_____

12) What are some specific and concrete safeguards against a prideful spirit? How can you implement those practices today?

_____

_____

_____

Recording Your Thoughts

_____

_____

For further study, see the following passages:

Genesis 41:39–45   Proverbs 15:25; 21:4; 29:23   Jeremiah 14:3–4
1 Corinthians 10:12   James 4:6

Haman's Downfall

Opening Thought

1) Rank the following in terms of how unfair they are (1 is the absolute worst injustice; 10 is the least):

_____ getting a ticket for going six miles over the speed limit when all other drivers have been passing you!

_____ the obviously guilty murderer who gets off on a legal technicality

_____ the wealthy neighbor who is the constant recipient of freebies, give-aways, and prizes

_____ the friend who never exercises or counts calories and still never gains an ounce

_____ getting passed over for a promotion because the boss wanted to hire her daughter-in-law

_____ the corrupt politician with lots of money who uses dirty tactics and misleading ads to defeat an honest challenger

_____ the convict who spends eleven years in prison for a crime he didn't commit

_____ the company that lays off a batch of loyal, lifelong employees in their late fifties

_____ a major network's refusal to report an important pro-life event or to accept a paid pro-life advertisement

_____ a judge who rules that a public school teacher cannot say, "Thank you, Jesus!" in the classroom

2) What are some of the greatest injustices you've witnessed in your life?

_____

_____

_____

3) What causes movie audiences to spontaneously cheer and applaud when the villain gets what he or she deserves?

_____

_____

_____

Background of the Passage

"That's not fair!"

This expression is one of the most common utterances of modern everyday discourse. Early in life, children gain a clear understanding of the concept of justice. And for the rest of our lives, we bump daily into situations that cry out for impartial assessment. Will right behavior be rewarded? We innately know it should be. Will wrong actions be judged as such? Will the people who do evil have to face the music? Something in us longs for the even-handed application of both reward and punishment.

In Esther's story, a hot-headed and prideful man named Haman was rewarded for his evil actions (7:1–8:2). He had been plotting genocide against the Jewish people living in Persia. With his high rank, and with the apparent blessing of King Ahasuerus, his murderous dream seemed destined to come to pass.

The sovereign God had other plans, however. The new queen of Persia happened to be Esther, a Jewish woman herself, and her cousin Mordecai was the same man who earlier had foiled an assassination plot on the king's life. As these situations and facts came together, and came to light, Haman's brutal plans caught up with him. The tables were turned. Justice was served.

What a good reminder that the Lord sees all and will one day make everything right.

Bible Passage

Read 7:1—8:2, noting the key words and definitions to the right of the passage.

Esther 7:1—8:2

1 *So the king and Haman went to dine with Queen Esther.*

2 *And on the second day, at the banquet of wine, the king again said to Esther, "What is your petition, Queen Esther? It shall be granted you. And what is your request, up to half the kingdom? It shall be done!"*

3 *Then Queen Esther answered and said, "If I have found favor in your sight, O king, and if it pleases the king, let my life be given me at my petition, and my people at my request.*

4 *For we have been sold, my people and I, to be destroyed, to be killed, and to be annihilated. Had we been sold as male and female slaves, I would have held my tongue, although the enemy could never compensate for the king's loss."*

5 *So King Ahasuerus answered and said to Queen Esther, "Who is he, and where is he, who would dare presume in his heart to do such a thing?"*

6 *And Esther said, "The adversary and enemy is this wicked Haman!" So Haman was terrified before the king and queen.*

7 *Then the king arose in his wrath from the banquet of wine and went into the palace garden; but Haman stood before Queen Esther, pleading for his life, for he saw that evil was determined against him by the king.*

8 *When the king returned from the palace garden to the place of the banquet of wine, Haman had fallen across the couch where Esther was. Then the king said, "Will he also assault the queen while I am in the house?" As the word left the king's mouth, they covered Haman's face.*

9 *Now Harbonah, one of the eunuchs, said to the king, "Look! The gallows, fifty cubits high, which Haman made for Mordecai, who spoke good on the king's behalf, is standing at the house of Haman." Then the king said, "Hang him on it!"*

10 *So they hanged Haman on the gallows that he*

second day (v. 2)—The first day reference point included the first banquet; this refers to the second banquet on the second day (see 5:8).

what is your request? (v. 2) —This was the third time that the king inquired (see 5:3, 6).

my people (v. 3)—This plea parallels God's message given to Pharaoh through Moses, "Let my people go," almost a thousand years earlier (Exodus 7:16).

sold (v. 4)—refers back to Haman's bribe (see 3:9; 4:7)

destroyed . . . killed . . . annihilated (v. 4)—Esther recounted the exact language of Haman's decree (see 3:13).

this wicked Haman (v. 6)— similar to Nathan's famous accusation against King David, "You are the man" (2 Samuel 12:7); Haman's honor quickly turned to humiliation and then to horror

assault the queen (v. 8)— Blinded by anger, Ahasuerus interpreted Haman's plea to be an act of violence against Esther rather than a plea for mercy.

Harbonah (v. 9)—See 1:10.

Look! (v. 9)—Because the place prepared by Haman for Mordecai's execution towered above the city, it was the obvious spot for Haman's death.

Mordecai, who spoke good (v. 9)—Haman heard the three capital offenses charged against him. One, he manipulated the king in planning to kill the queen's people. Two, he was perceived to accost the queen. Three, he planned to execute a man whom the king had just greatly honored

had prepared for Mordecai. Then the king's wrath subsided.

8:1 On that day King Ahasuerus gave Queen Esther the house of Haman, the enemy of the Jews. And Mordecai came before the king, for Esther had told how he was related to her.

² So the king took off his signet ring, which he had taken from Haman, and gave it to Mordecai; and Esther appointed Mordecai over the house of Haman.

for extreme loyalty to the kingdom.

they hanged Haman (v. 10)—the ultimate expression of justice (see Psalm 9:15–16)

the house of Haman (8:1)—The property of a traitor by Persian custom returned to the king. In this case, the king gave it to his queen, Esther, who put Mordecai in charge of it (8:2). The fate of Haman's wife, Zeresh, and his wise men is unknown (5:14; 6:12–13). Haman's ten sons later died (9:7–10).

Understanding the Text

4) When Esther finally made her request to the king, how did the king react? How did Haman react?

_____

_____

_____

_____

_____

5) How was Ahasuerus an instrument of God?

_____

_____

_____

_____

_____

_____

(verses to consider: Proverbs 21:1; Habakkuk 1:6; Isaiah 45:1)

6) How was Mordecai exalted?

_____

_____

_____

_____

_____

(verses to consider: Genesis 41:41–45; Daniel 2:46–49)

Cross-Reference

Read Psalm 37.

¹ *Do not fret because of evildoers, nor be envious of the workers of iniquity.*

² *For they shall soon be cut down like the grass, and wither as the green herb.*

³ *Trust in the LORD, and do good; dwell in the land, and feed on His faithfulness.*

⁴ *Delight yourself also in the LORD, and He shall give you the desires of your heart.*

⁵ *Commit your way to the LORD, trust also in Him, and He shall bring it to pass.*

⁶ *He shall bring forth your righteousness as the light, and your justice as the noonday.*

⁷ *Rest in the LORD, and wait patiently for Him; do not fret because of him who prospers in his way, because of the man who brings wicked schemes to pass.*

⁸ *Cease from anger, and forsake wrath; do not fret—it only causes harm.*

⁹ *For evildoers shall be cut off; but those who wait on the LORD, they shall inherit the earth.*

¹⁰ *For yet a little while and the wicked shall be no more; indeed, you will look carefully for his place, but it shall be no more.*

¹¹ *But the meek shall inherit the earth, and shall delight themselves in the abundance of peace.*

¹² *The wicked plots against the just, and gnashes at him with his teeth.*

¹³ *The LORD laughs at him, for He sees that his day is coming.*

¹⁴ *The wicked have drawn the sword and have bent their bow, to cast down the poor and needy, to slay those who are of upright conduct.*

¹⁵ *Their sword shall enter their own heart, and their bows shall be broken.*

¹⁶ *A little that a righteous man has is better than the riches of many wicked.*

¹⁷ *For the arms of the wicked shall be broken, but the* LORD *upholds the righteous.*

¹⁸ *The* LORD *knows the days of the upright, and their inheritance shall be forever.*

¹⁹ *They shall not be ashamed in the evil time, and in the days of famine they shall be satisfied.*

²⁰ *But the wicked shall perish; and the enemies of the* LORD, *like the splendor of the meadows, shall vanish. Into smoke they shall vanish away.*

²¹ *The wicked borrows and does not repay, but the righteous shows mercy and gives.*

²² *For those blessed by Him shall inherit the earth, but those cursed by Him shall be cut off.*

²³ *The steps of a good man are ordered by the* LORD, *and He delights in his way.*

²⁴ *Though he fall, he shall not be utterly cast down; for the* LORD *upholds him with His hand.*

²⁵ *I have been young, and now am old; yet I have not seen the righteous forsaken, nor his descendants begging bread.*

²⁶ *He is ever merciful, and lends; and his descendants are blessed.*

²⁷ *Depart from evil, and do good; and dwell forevermore.*

²⁸ *For the* LORD *loves justice, and does not forsake His saints; They are preserved forever, But the descendants of the wicked shall be cut off.*

²⁹ *The righteous shall inherit the land, and dwell in it forever.*

³⁰ *The mouth of the righteous speaks wisdom, and his tongue talks of justice.*

³¹ *The law of his God is in his heart; none of his steps shall slide.*

³² *The wicked watches the righteous, and seeks to slay him.*

³³ *The* LORD *will not leave him in his hand, nor condemn him when he is judged.*

³⁴ *Wait on the* LORD, *and keep His way, and He shall exalt you to inherit the land; when the wicked are cut off, you shall see it.*

³⁵ *I have seen the wicked in great power, and spreading himself like a native green tree.*

³⁶ *Yet he passed away, and behold, he was no more; indeed I sought him, but he could not be found.*

³⁷ *Mark the blameless man, and observe the upright; for the future of that man is peace.*

³⁸ *But the transgressors shall be destroyed together; the future of the wicked shall be cut off.*

³⁹ *But the salvation of the righteous is from the* LORD; *He is their strength in the time of trouble.*

⁴⁰ *And the* LORD *shall help them and deliver them; He shall deliver them from the wicked, and save them, because they trust in Him.*

7) What does David's psalm say with certainty about the destinies of the wicked and the righteous? Do we always see ultimate justice in this life?

_____

_____

_____

_____

_____

_____

8) Read Isaiah 13:11. How does its statement regarding the punishment of the wicked dovetail with the declarations of Psalm 37?

_____

_____

_____

_____

_____

_____

(verses to consider: Psalm 145:20; Proverbs 21:7)

Exploring the Meaning

9) Go back and underline every statement about the destruction of the wicked found in Psalm 37.

_____

_____

_____

_____

_____

10) Read Deuteronomy 32:4. What does it tell you about the nature of God?

_____

_____

_____

_____

_____

(verses to consider: Psalms 37:28; 89:14)

11) Circle every promise to the faithful in Psalm 37.

_____

_____

_____

_____

_____

Summing Up...

"The wonder is not that God promises to condemn sinners for their sin but that He first offers them deliverance from it. In coming to save those who trust in Him, the Lord Jesus Christ demonstrated His great love for the unlovely by bearing the penalty of their sin, dying the death they deserve. What is remarkable is that He came to redeem sinners who are worthy only of His judgment."—*John MacArthur*

Reflecting on the Text

12) As you look around you and see unbelievers who do not honor God and yet who seem to be prospering in life, how can (and should) this passage from Esther alter your attitudes?

_____

_____

_____

_____

_____

_____

13) How is Mordecai's life a challenge to you to be faithful no matter what the circumstances?

_____

_____

_____

_____

_____

_____

14) God had placed Esther in her unique position of influence "for such a time as this." What unique opportunities or platforms has God given you? List two or three specific things you could do this week to use your position for the glory of God and the good of Christ's church.

_____

_____

_____

_____

_____

_____

Recording Your Thoughts

_____
_____
_____
_____
_____
_____
_____
_____
_____
_____
_____
_____
_____
_____
_____
_____
_____
_____
_____
_____
_____
_____

For further study, see the following passages:

| Genesis 18:25 | Exodus 7:16 | 2 Samuel 12:7 |
| Psalm 7:11; 73 | Proverbs 21:15 | |

The Jews' Deliverance

Opening Thought

1) Describe a time in your life when you were expecting one thing and the exact opposite happened. Were you more surprised, shocked, glad, sad, or mad?

_____

_____

_____

2) What is a "comeback"? What's the most amazing comeback or seemingly impossible turnaround you've ever witnessed?

_____

_____

_____

3) Why do the media get so enamored with comebacks (whether political, athletic, or economic)?

_____

_____

_____

_____

Background of the Passage

Though God is not mentioned by name in this book, He was clearly at work in Esther's life and in the situation.

In the first seven chapters God
1. engineered circumstances so that Esther, a beautiful young Jewish woman, would become queen of all Persia, in the place of the deposed Vashti;
2. orchestrated events so that Esther's Cousin Mordecai would be a candidate for royal favor because of his discovery and reporting of an assassination plot against the king;
3. allowed the prideful Haman to concoct a seemingly airtight scheme to eradicate the Jewish people;
4. made the king agreeable to hear and comply with Esther's desperate petition for her people's deliverance;
5. kept the king from sleeping, only to remind him of Mordecai's earlier act of loyalty;
6. forced Haman to honor Mordecai before having Haman executed.

Following the death of their mortal foe, the Jews received even more good news. A counterdecree was approved by Ahasuerus, giving Mordecai and the exile community the authority to protect themselves by punishing any and all enemies. The result was that more than five hundred Persian men were killed by the Jews in Shushan alone, including Haman's ten sons.

What an amazing turn of events! A dark and bleak situation—with no hope in sight. But God was faithful, working in and through His faithful servants. The result? A true miracle! A good reminder of God's proclamation in Isaiah 55:8–9: "'For My thoughts are not your thoughts, nor are your ways My ways,' says the LORD 'For as the heavens are higher than the earth, so are My ways higher than your ways, and My thoughts than your thoughts.'"

Bible Passage

Read 8:3—9:19, noting the key words and definitions to the right of the passage.

Esther 8:3—9:19
3 Now Esther spoke again to the king, fell down at his feet, and implored him with tears to counteract the evil of Haman the Agagite, and the scheme which he had devised against the Jews.

⁴ *And the king held out the golden scepter toward Esther. So Esther arose and stood before the king,*

⁵ *and said, "If it pleases the king, and if I have found favor in his sight and the thing seems right to the king and I am pleasing in his eyes, let it be written to revoke the letters devised by Haman, the son of Hammedatha the Agagite, which he wrote to annihilate the Jews who are in all the king's provinces.*

⁶ *For how can I endure to see the evil that will come to my people? Or how can I endure to see the destruction of my countrymen?"*

⁷ *Then King Ahasuerus said to Queen Esther and Mordecai the Jew, "Indeed, I have given Esther the house of Haman, and they have hanged him on the gallows because he tried to lay his hand on the Jews.*

⁸ *You yourselves write a decree concerning the Jews, as you please, in the king's name, and seal it with the king's signet ring; for whatever is written in the king's name and sealed with the king's signet ring no one can revoke."*

⁹ *So the king's scribes were called at that time, in the third month, which is the month of Sivan, on the twenty-third day; and it was written, according to all that Mordecai commanded, to the Jews, the satraps, the governors, and the princes of the provinces from India to Ethiopia, one hundred and twenty-seven provinces in all, to every province in its own script, to every people in their own language, and to the Jews in their own script and language.*

¹⁰ *And he wrote in the name of King Ahasuerus, sealed it with the king's signet ring, and sent letters by couriers on horseback, riding on royal horses bred from swift steeds.*

¹¹ *By these letters the king permitted the Jews who were in every city to gather together and protect their lives—to destroy, kill, and annihilate all the forces of any people or province that would*

to revoke (v. 5)—This proved to be impossible in light of the inflexible nature of the king's edicts (1:19); however, counterdecree was possible (see 8:8, 11–12).

Sivan (v. 9)—This refers to the period May–June. It had been two months and ten days since Haman's decree (see 3:12); eight months and twenty days remained until both decrees became simultaneously effective (see 3:13).

the king permitted (v. 11)—Just as the king had permitted Haman, so he permitted the Jews to defend themselves and to plunder their spoil (see 9:10, 15, 16).

assault them, both little children and women, and to plunder their possessions,

12 on one day in all the provinces of King Ahasuerus, on the thirteenth day of the twelfth month, which is the month of Adar.

13 A copy of the document was to be issued as a decree in every province and published for all people, so that the Jews would be ready on that day to avenge themselves on their enemies.

14 The couriers who rode on royal horses went out, hastened and pressed on by the king's command. And the decree was issued in Shushan the citadel.

15 So Mordecai went out from the presence of the king in royal apparel of blue and white, with a great crown of gold and a garment of fine linen and purple; and the city of Shushan rejoiced and was glad.

16 The Jews had light and gladness, joy and honor.

17 And in every province and city, wherever the king's command and decree came, the Jews had joy and gladness, a feast and a holiday. Then many of the people of the land became Jews, because fear of the Jews fell upon them.

9:1 Now in the twelfth month, that is, the month of Adar, on the thirteenth day, the time came for the king's command and his decree to be executed. On the day that the enemies of the Jews had hoped to overpower them, the opposite occurred, in that the Jews themselves overpowered those who hated them.

2 The Jews gathered together in their cities throughout all the provinces of King Ahasuerus to lay hands on those who sought their harm. And no one could withstand them, because fear of them fell upon all people.

3 And all the officials of the provinces, the satraps, the governors, and all those doing the king's work, helped the Jews, because the fear of Mordecai fell upon them.

Mordecai went out (v. 15)—This second reward exceeded the first (see 6:6-9); blue and white were the royal colors of the Persian Empire.

many . . . people . . . Jews (v. 17)—The population realized that the God of the Jews greatly exceeded anything that the pantheon of Persian deities could offer (see Exodus 15:14–16), especially in contrast to their recent defeat by the Greeks.

twelfth month (9:1)—during the period February–March; here is a powerful statement with regard to God's providential preservation of the Jewish race in harmony with God's unconditional promise to Abraham (Genesis 17:1–8); this providential deliverance stands in contrast to God's miraculous deliverance of the Jews from Egypt; yet in both cases the same end had been accomplished by the supernatural power of God.

the fear of Mordecai (v. 3)—Pragmatically, the nation had a change of heart toward the Jews, knowing that the king, the queen, and Mordecai were the ranking royal officials of the land. To be pro-Jewish would put one in favor with the king and his court and

⁴ *For Mordecai was great in the king's palace, and his fame spread throughout all the provinces; for this man Mordecai became increasingly prominent.*

⁵ *Thus the Jews defeated all their enemies with the stroke of the sword, with slaughter and destruction, and did what they pleased with those who hated them.*

⁶ *And in Shushan the citadel the Jews killed and destroyed five hundred men.*

⁷ *Also Parshandatha, Dalphon, Aspatha,*

⁸ *Poratha, Adalia, Aridatha,*

⁹ *Parmashta, Arisai, Aridai, and Vajezatha—*

¹⁰ *the ten sons of Haman the son of Hammedatha, the enemy of the Jews—they killed; but they did not lay a hand on the plunder.*

¹¹ *On that day the number of those who were killed in Shushan the citadel was brought to the king.*

¹² *And the king said to Queen Esther, "The Jews have killed and destroyed five hundred men in Shushan the citadel, and the ten sons of Haman. What have they done in the rest of the king's provinces? Now what is your petition? It shall be granted to you. Or what is your further request? It shall be done."*

¹³ *Then Esther said, "If it pleases the king, let it be granted to the Jews who are in Shushan to do again tomorrow according to today's decree, and let Haman's ten sons be hanged on the gallows."*

¹⁴ *So the king commanded this to be done; the decree was issued in Shushan, and they hanged Haman's ten sons.*

¹⁵ *And the Jews who were in Shushan gathered together again on the fourteenth day of the month of Adar and killed three hundred men at Shushan; but they did not lay a hand on the plunder.*

¹⁶ *The remainder of the Jews in the king's provinces gathered together and protected their lives, had rest from their enemies, and killed seventy-five*

put one on the side of God, the ultimate King (see Revelation 19:16).

did not lay a hand (v. 10)—Unlike Saul, who did take the plunder (see 1 Samuel 15:3 with 15:9), the Jews focused only on the mission at hand, that is, to preserve the Jewish race (see 9:15–16), even though the king's edict permitted this (8:11).

further request? (v. 12)—Even this pagan king served the cause of utterly blotting out the Amalekites in accord with God's original decree.(Exodus 17:14) by allowing for a second day of killing in Shushan to eliminate all Jewish enemies.

be hanged (v. 13)—be publicly displayed

fourteenth day (v. 15)—Another 300 men died the second day of killing in Shushan, bringing the total dead in Shushan to 810.

had rest from their enemies (v. 16)—Over fifteen hundred years earlier God had promised to curse those who curse Abraham's descendants (Genesis 12:3).

killed (v. 16)—Outside of Shushan, only one day of killing occurred in which seventy-five thousand enemies died.

thousand of their enemies; but they did not lay a hand on the plunder.

17 This was on the thirteenth day of the month of Adar. And on the fourteenth day of the month they rested and made it a day of feasting and gladness.

18 But the Jews who were at Shushan assembled together on the thirteenth day, as well as on the fourteenth; and on the fifteenth of the month they rested, and made it a day of feasting and gladness.

19 Therefore the Jews of the villages who dwelt in the unwalled towns celebrated the fourteenth day of the month of Adar with gladness and feasting, as a holiday, and for sending presents to one another.

as well as on the fourteenth (v. 18)——would be celebrated for two days rather than one.

Understanding the Text

4) What steps led to the revocation of Haman's decree?

_____

_____

_____

_____

5) What kind of decree did Ahasuerus allow Mordecai to make on behalf of the Jewish people (see 8:11)? What effect did this decree have on the Jewish people?

_____

_____

_____

_____

_____

6) How did these events affect the Persian populace?

_____

_____

_____

_____

_____

(verses to consider: Leviticus 26:8; Deuteronomy 2:25; Joshua 23:10)

Cross-Reference

Read Revelation 19:11—20:10.

11 *Now I saw heaven opened, and behold, a white horse. And He who sat on him was called Faithful and True, and in righteousness He judges and makes war.*

12 *His eyes were like a flame of fire, and on His head were many crowns. He had a name written that no one knew except Himself.*

13 *He was clothed with a robe dipped in blood, and His name is called The Word of God.*

14 *And the armies in heaven, clothed in fine linen, white and clean, followed Him on white horses.*

15 *Now out of His mouth goes a sharp sword, that with it He should strike the nations. And He Himself will rule them with a rod of iron. He Himself treads the winepress of the fierceness and wrath of Almighty God.*

16 *And He has on His robe and on His thigh a name written: KING OF KINGS AND LORD OF LORDS.*

17 *Then I saw an angel standing in the sun; and he cried with a loud voice, saying to all the birds that fly in the midst of heaven, "Come and gather together for the supper of the great God,*

18 *that you may eat the flesh of kings, the flesh of captains, the flesh of mighty men, the flesh of horses and of those who sit on them, and the flesh of all people, free and slave, both small and great."*

19 *And I saw the beast, the kings of the earth, and their armies, gathered together to make war against Him who sat on the horse and against His army.*

20 *Then the beast was captured, and with him the false prophet who worked signs in his presence, by which he deceived those who received the mark of the beast*

and those who worshiped his image. These two were cast alive into the lake of fire burning with brimstone.

21 And the rest were killed with the sword which proceeded from the mouth of Him who sat on the horse. And all the birds were filled with their flesh.

20:1 Then I saw an angel coming down from heaven, having the key to the bottomless pit and a great chain in his hand.

2 He laid hold of the dragon, that serpent of old, who is the Devil and Satan, and bound him for a thousand years;

3 and he cast him into the bottomless pit, and shut him up, and set a seal on him, so that he should deceive the nations no more till the thousand years were finished. But after these things he must be released for a little while.

4 And I saw thrones, and they sat on them, and judgment was committed to them. Then I saw the souls of those who had been beheaded for their witness to Jesus and for the word of God, who had not worshiped the beast or his image, and had not received his mark on their foreheads or on their hands. And they lived and reigned with Christ for a thousand years.

5 But the rest of the dead did not live again until the thousand years were finished. This is the first resurrection.

6 Blessed and holy is he who has part in the first resurrection. Over such the second death has no power, but they shall be priests of God and of Christ, and shall reign with Him a thousand years.

7 Now when the thousand years have expired, Satan will be released from his prison

8 and will go out to deceive the nations which are in the four corners of the earth, Gog and Magog, to gather them together to battle, whose number is as the sand of the sea.

9 They went up on the breadth of the earth and surrounded the camp of the saints and the beloved city. And fire came down from God out of heaven and devoured them.

10 The devil, who deceived them, was cast into the lake of fire and brimstone where the beast and the false prophet are. And they will be tormented day and night forever and ever.

7) What does this passage say about the ultimate overthrow of the enemies of God and God's people?

_____

_____

_____

_____

_____

Exploring the Meaning

8) Read 1 Thessalonians 1:9–10. How were the Thessalonians similar to the Jewish converts of Esther 8:17?

_____

_____

_____

(verses to consider: Jonah 3:5–10; Acts 5:11–14)

9) Some people of faith argue that total trust in God means it is never right to defend oneself against the charges or attacks of the wicked. What do you think about this argument and about Mordecai's decree?

_____

_____

_____

_____

Summing Up...

"Through the centuries . . . men have shaken their fists in defiance at God. And though the folly of fighting Him is self-evident, that does not stop each succeeding generation from trying. They pit their impotence against His omnipotence, shattering themselves like raw eggs thrown against granite. . . . Though sinful men often hail those who fight against God as wise, in reality they are fools. True wisdom lies in being on God's side."—*John MacArthur*

Reflecting on the Text

10) Can you think of an area in your life in which all seems hopeless? How does the story of Esther and Mordecai alter the way in which you think about this situation?

_____

_____

_____

_____

11) Consider those individuals in your life who need to see God work an amazing comeback. How can you come alongside them in their time of need? What specific acts of encouragement could you perform?

_____

_____

_____

_____

Recording Your Thoughts

_____

_____

_____

_____

_____

_____

For further study, see the following passages:

Genesis 12:3   Exodus 17:14   Deuteronomy 1:30
Psalm 105:38   Revelation 19:16

The Jews' Celebration

Opening Thought

1) What is your favorite holiday of the year and why?

_____

_____

_____

2) Describe the worship at your church. What are your personal
habits of worship? Are they occasions of true celebration and
unabashed joy, or something else?

_____

_____

_____

_____

3) When was the last time you genuinely celebrated? What
prompted this occasion?

_____

_____

_____

_____

_____

Background of the Passage

Some cynic has quipped that there is no such thing as a happy ending. He or she obviously has never read the Book of Esther.

Like a first-rate suspense novel, this true narrative of the Jews who remained in Persia following the exile takes the reader on an emotional roller-coaster ride. From surprise to despair and from fear to triumph, Esther records how the invisible (but powerful!) hand of God protected His people and provided great blessing for them in a foreign land.

At the conclusion of the book, we find the Jewish people engaged in a great celebration, the Feast of Purim. This festival commemorated their miraculous preservation from the genocidal plot of Haman. Purim is a holiday still celebrated by the Jewish faithful to this day.

How did this unlikely holiday come about? Esther's charm and beauty won the king's heart. Mordecai's honesty and wisdom won the king's gratitude. When the crisis arose, therefore, this God-fearing tandem was able to use their position and influence to make a life and death difference. The Jewish people were spared; the glory of God was revealed.

This book is packed with powerful lessons, but one moral of the story is this: The faithful who participate in the work of God will eventually see and celebrate the wonders of God.

Bible Passage

Read 9:20—10:3, noting the key words and definitions to the right of the passage.

Esther 9:20—10:3

²⁰ *And Mordecai wrote these things and sent letters to all the Jews, near and far, who were in all the provinces of King Ahasuerus,*

²¹ *to establish among them that they should celebrate yearly the fourteenth and fifteenth days of the month of Adar,*

²² *as the days on which the Jews had rest from their*

And Mordecai wrote these things (vv. 20-25)—a brief summary of God's providential intervention on behalf of the Jews

enemies, as the month which was turned from sorrow to joy for them, and from mourning to a holiday; that they should make them days of feasting and joy, of sending presents to one another and gifts to the poor.

23 So the Jews accepted the custom which they had begun, as Mordecai had written to them,

24 because Haman, the son of Hammedatha the Agagite, the enemy of all the Jews, had plotted against the Jews to annihilate them, and had cast Pur (that is, the lot), to consume them and destroy them;

25 but when Esther came before the king, he commanded by letter that this wicked plot which Haman had devised against the Jews should return on his own head, and that he and his sons should be hanged on the gallows.

26 So they called these days Purim, after the name Pur. Therefore, because of all the words of this letter, what they had seen concerning this matter, and what had happened to them,

27 the Jews established and imposed it upon themselves and their descendants and all who would join them, that without fail they should celebrate these two days every year, according to the written instructions and according to the prescribed time,

28 that these days should be remembered and kept throughout every generation, every family, every province, and every city, that these days of Purim should not fail to be observed among the Jews, and that the memory of them should not perish among their descendants.

29 Then Queen Esther, the daughter of Abihail, with Mordecai the Jew, wrote with full authority to confirm this second letter about Purim.

30 And Mordecai sent letters to all the Jews, to the one hundred and twenty-seven provinces of the kingdom of Ahasuerus, with words of peace and truth,

Purim (v. 26)—the only biblically revealed, non-Mosaic festival with perpetual significance

second letter (v. 29)—an additional letter (see verse 20 for the first letter), which added "fasting and lamenting" to the prescribed activity of Purim

31 to confirm these days of Purim at their appointed time, as Mordecai the Jew and Queen Esther had prescribed for them, and as they had decreed for themselves and their descendants concerning matters of their fasting and lamenting.

32 So the decree of Esther confirmed these matters of Purim, and it was written in the book.

10:1 And King Ahasuerus imposed tribute on the land and on the islands of the sea.

2 Now all the acts of his power and his might, and the account of the greatness of Mordecai, to which the king advanced him, are they not written in the book of the chronicles of the kings of Media and Persia?

3 For Mordecai the Jew was second to King Ahasuerus, and was great among the Jews and well received by the multitude of his brethren, seeking the good of his people and speaking peace to all his countrymen.

written in the book (v. 32)— This could be the chronicle referred to in 10:3 or another archival type document; it certainly does not hint that Esther wrote this canonical book.

And King Ahasuerus imposed tribute (vv. 1-3)—apparently a postscript

Mordecai . . . was second (v. 3)—Mordecai joined the top echelon of Jewish international statesmen like Joseph, who ranked second in the Egyptian dynasty (Genesis 41:37–45), and Daniel, who succeeded in both the Babylonian (Daniel 5:29) and Medo-Persian Empires (Daniel 6:28).

speaking peace (v. 3)— Ahasuerus was assassinated. No further details are available concerning Esther and Mordecai. What Mordecai did for less than a decade on behalf of Israel, Jesus Christ will do for all eternity as the Prince of Peace (Isaiah 9:6–7; Zechariah 9:9–10).

Understanding the Text

4) According to the description in this passage, what sorts of things did the Jews do to celebrate the Feast of Purim?

_____

_____

_____

_____

5) The Pur (or lots) that Haman had cast as part of his scheme to annihilate the Jews eventually became a symbol, not of death and destruction, but of God's goodness and power. How? Can you think of other negative symbols that ironically have come to serve as positive reminders?

_____

_____

_____

_____

_____

_____

6) At the end of this book, how is Mordecai described? What does this reveal about God's ability to place His people in positions of strategic importance?

_____

_____

_____

_____

(verses to consider: Psalm 147:6; Proverbs 8:15; Romans 13:1)

Cross-Reference

Read Psalm 47.

¹ *Oh, clap your hands, all you peoples! Shout to God with the voice of triumph!*
² *For the LORD Most High is awesome; He is a great King over all the earth.*
³ *He will subdue the peoples under us, and the nations under our feet.*
⁴ *He will choose our inheritance for us, the excellence of Jacob whom He loves. Selah*
⁵ *God has gone up with a shout, the LORD with the sound of a trumpet.*
⁶ *Sing praises to God, sing praises! Sing praises to our King, sing praises!*
⁷ *For God is the King of all the earth; sing praises with understanding.*
⁸ *God reigns over the nations; God sits on His holy throne.*
⁹ *The princes of the people have gathered together, the people of the God of Abraham. For the shields of the earth belong to God; He is greatly exalted.*

7) What is the theme or message of Psalm 47 and why would this have been an appropriate song of praise for the Jews in Persia to sing?

_____

_____

_____

_____

_____

Exploring the Meaning

8) Read Exodus 15:1–21. What specific deliverance was being celebrated here? What common elements do you see in the celebration of the Jews at Purim and the Jews at the Red Sea?

_____

_____

_____

_____

_____

9) Read Revelation 7:9–17. What does the scene pictured in this passage teach about God? About appropriate worship on the part of the people of God?

_____

_____

_____

_____

Summing Up...

"Genuine worship is the supreme service a Christian can offer to Christ. There is a time for ministering to the poor, the sick, the naked, and the imprisoned. There is a time for witnessing to the lost and seeking to lead them to the Savior. There is a time for discipling new believers and helping them grow in the faith. There is a time for careful study and teaching of God's Word. But above all else that the Lord requires of His people is true worship, without which everything else they may do in His name is empty and powerless."—*John MacArthur*

Reflecting on the Text

10) As you think about the religious days Christians celebrate (Easter, Thanksgiving, Christmas), are they *holy days* to you? Or mere secularized *holidays?* Why? What needs to change?

_____

_____

_____

_____

_____

11) What, specifically, could you do today to celebrate and commemorate God's goodness and deliverance?

_____

_____

_____

_____

_____

12) A friend comes to you and says, "I have no joy in worship. It has become nothing more than a time of dry, dull ritual. What should I do?" What counsel would you give?

_____

_____

_____

13) What is one thing you'd like to change about your habits of worship?

_____

_____

_____

14) What lessons or truths from Esther have had the biggest impact on you personally? Why?

_____

_____

_____

_____

Recording Your Thoughts

_____

_____

_____

For further study, see the following passages:

Genesis 41:37–45   Judges 5   1 Chronicles 16
Isaiah 9:6   Daniel 2:46–49

The MacArthur Bible Collection

John MacArthur, General Editor

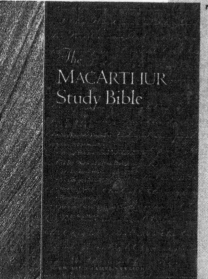

The MacArthur Study Bible

From the moment you pick it up, you'll know it's a classic. Featuring the word-for-word accuracy of the New King James Version, *The MacArthur Study Bible* is perfect for serious study. Pastor/teacher John MacArthur has compiled more than 20,000 study notes, a 200-page topical index and numerous charts, maps, outlines, and articles to create *The MacArthur Study Bible*. This Bible has been crafted with the finest materials in a variety of handsome bindings, including hardcover and indexed bonded leather. Winner of "The 1998 Study Bible of the Year Award."

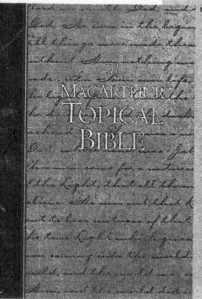

The MacArthur Topical Bible

In the excellent tradition of *Nave's Topical Bible*, this newly created reference book incorporates thousands of topics and ideas, both traditional and contemporary, for believers today and in the new millennium. Carefully researched and prepared by Dr. John MacArthur and the faculty of Masters Seminary, *The MacArthur Topical Bible* will quickly become the reference of choice of all serious Bible students. Using the New King James translation, this Bible is arranged alphabetically by topic and is completely cross-referenced. This exhaustive resource is an indispensible tool for the topical study of God's Word.

The MacArthur Bible Studies

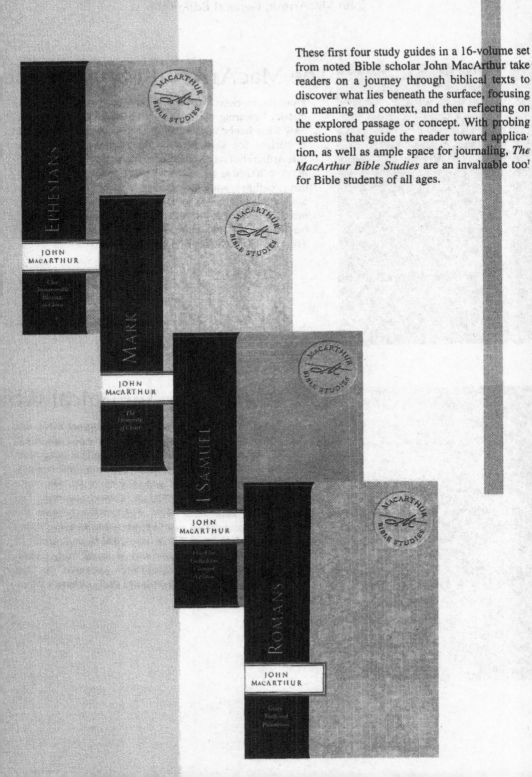

These first four study guides in a 16-volume set from noted Bible scholar John MacArthur take readers on a journey through biblical texts to discover what lies beneath the surface, focusing on meaning and context, and then reflecting on the explored passage or concept. With probing questions that guide the reader toward application, as well as ample space for journaling, *The MacArthur Bible Studies* are an invaluable tool for Bible students of all ages.